BEST-SELLING
HOUSE PLANS
UPDATED & REVISED
5TH EDITION

Book content provided by Design America, Inc., St. Louis, MO.

Printed in China
First Printing

Best-Selling House Plans, 5th Edition
ISBN-13: 978-1-58011-590-2

Library of Congress Control Number: 2023923012

CREATIVE HOMEOWNER®
www.creativehomeowner.com

Creative Homeowner books are distributed by

Fox Chapel Publishing
903 Square Street
Mount Joy, PA 17552
www.FoxChapelPublishing.com

The main home on the cover is Plan #F13-091D-0509 on page 23; Bottom, left to right: Plan #F13-091D-0534 on page 101 and Plan #F13-011D-0684 on page 38.

CONTENTS

Top to bottom: Plan #F13-101D-0056 on page 123, Warren Diggles Photography; Plan #F13-011D-0013 on page 19; Plan #F13-051D-0970, on page 104; Plan #F13-123D-0056 on page 26; Plan #F13-011D-0347 on page 155; Plan #F13-026D-1876 on page 17.

what's the right PLAN for you?

Choosing a house design is exciting, but can be a difficult task. Many factors play a role in what home plan is best for you and your family. To help you get started, we have pinpointed some of the major factors to consider when searching for your dream home. Take the time to evaluate your family's needs and you will have an easier time sorting through all of the house designs offered in this book.

BUDGET is the first thing to consider. Many items take part in this budget, from ordering the blueprints to the last doorknob purchased. When you find the perfect house plan, visit houseplansandmore.com and get a cost-to-build estimate to ensure that the finished home will be within your cost range. A cost-to-build report is a detailed summary that gives you the total cost to build a specific home in the zip code where you're wanting to build. It is interactive allowing you to adjust labor and material costs, and it's created on

demand when ordered so all pricing is up-to-date. This valuable tool will help you know how much your dream home will cost before you buy plans (see page 186 for more information).

FAMILY LIFESTYLE After your budget is deciphered, you need to assess you and your family's lifestyle needs. Think about the stage of life you are in now, and what stages you will be going through in the future. Ask yourself questions to figure out how much room you need now and if you will need room for expansion. Are you married? Do you have children? How many children do you plan on having? Are you an empty-nester? How long do you plan to live in this home?

Incorporate into your planning any frequent guests you may have, including elderly parents, grandchildren or adult children who may live with you.

Does your family entertain a lot? If so, think about the rooms you will need to do so. Will you need both formal and informal spaces? Do you need a gourmet kitchen? Do you need a game room and/or a wet bar?

FLOOR PLAN LAYOUTS When looking through these home plans, imagine yourself walking through the house. Consider the flow from the entry to the living, sleeping and gathering areas. Does the layout ensure privacy for the master bedroom? Does the garage enter near the kitchen for easy unloading? Does the placement of the windows provide enough privacy from any neigh-

boring properties? Do you plan on using furniture you already have? Will this furniture fit in the appropriate rooms? When you find a plan you want to purchase, be sure to picture yourself actually living in it.

EXTERIOR SPACES With many different home styles throughout ranging from Traditional to Contemporary, flip through these pages and find which best-selling home design appeals to you the most and think about the neighborhood in which you plan to build. Also, think about how the house will fit on your site. Picture the landscaping you want to add to the lot. Using your imagination is key when choosing a home plan.

Choosing a house design can be an intimidating experience. Asking yourself these questions before you get started on the search will help you through the process. With our large selection of sizes and styles, we are certain you will find your dream home in this book.

MAKE A LIST!

Experts in the field suggest that the best way to determine your needs is to begin by listing everything you like or dislike about your current home.

10 steps to BUILDING your dream home

1 talk to a lender

If you plan to obtain a loan in order to build your new home, then it's best to find out first how much you can get approved for before selecting a home design. Knowing the financial information before you start looking for land or a home will keep you from selecting something out of your budget and turning a great experience into a major disappointment. Financing the home you plan to build is somewhat different than financing the purchase of an existing house. You're going to need thousands of dollars for land, labor, and materials. Chances are, you're going to have to borrow most of it. Therefore, you will probably need to obtain a construction loan. This is a short-term loan to pay for building your house. When the house is completed, the loan is paid off in full, usually out of the proceeds from your long-term mortgage loan.

2 determine needs

Selecting the right home plan for your needs and lifestyle requires a lot of thought. Your new home is an investment, so you should consider not only your current needs, but also your future requirements. Versatility and the potential for converting certain areas to other uses could be an important factor later on. So, although a home office may seem unnecessary now, in years to come, the idea may seem ideal. Home plans that include flex spaces or bonus rooms can really adapt to your needs in the future.

3 choose a home site

The site for your new home will have a definite impact on the design you select. It's a good idea to select a home that will complement your site. This will save you time and money when building. Or, you can then modify a design to specifically accommodate your site. However, it will most likely make your home construction more costly than selecting a home plan suited for your lot right from the start. For example, if your land slopes, a walk-out basement works perfectly. If it's wooded, or has a lake in the back, an atrium ranch home is a perfect style to take advantage of surrounding backyard views.

SOME IMPORTANT CRITERIA TO CONSIDER WHEN SELECTING A SITE:

- Improvements will need to be made including utilities, sidewalks and driveways
- Convenience of the lot to work, school, shops, etc.
- Zoning requirements and property tax amounts
- Soil conditions at your future site
- Make sure the person or firm that sells you the land owns it free and clear

---

4 select a home design

The top-selling home plans found on houseplansandmore.com are featured in this book. With over 20,000 home plans from the best architects and designers across the country, this book includes the best variety of styles and sizes to suit the needs and tastes of a broad spectrum of homeowners.

5 get the cost to build

If you feel you have found "the" home, then before taking the step of purchasing house plans, order an estimated cost-to-build report for the exact zip code where you plan to build. Requesting this custom cost report created specifically for you will help educate you on all costs associated with building your new home. Simply order this report and gain knowledge of the material and labor cost associated with the home you love. Not only does the report allow you to choose the quality of the materials, you can also select options in every aspect of the project from lot condition to contractor fees. This report will allow you to successfully manage your construction budget in all areas, clearly see where the majority of the costs lie, and save you money from start to finish.

A COST-TO-BUILD REPORT WILL DETERMINE THE OVERALL COST OF YOUR NEW HOME INCLUDING THESE 5 MAJOR EXPENSE CATEGORIES:

- Land
- Foundation
- Materials
- General Contractor's fee - Some rules-of-thumb that you may find useful are: (a) the total labor cost will generally run a little higher than your total material cost, but it's not unusual for a builder or general contractor to charge 15-20% of the combined cost for managing the overall project.
- Site improvements - don't forget to add in the cost of your site improvements such as utilities, driveway, sidewalks, landscaping, etc.

6 hire a contractor

If you're inexperienced in construction, you'll probably want to hire a general contractor to manage the project. If you do not know a reputable general contractor, begin your search by contacting your local Home Builders Association to get references. Many states require building contractors to be licensed. If this is the case in your state, its licensing board is another referral source. Finding a reputable, quality-minded contractor is a key factor in ensuring that your new home is well constructed and is finished on time and within budget. It can be a smart decision to discuss the plan you like with your builder prior to ordering plans. They can guide you into choosing the right type of plan package option especially if you intend on doing some customizing to the design.

7 customizing

Sometimes your general contractor may want to be the one who makes the modifications you want to the home you've

selected. But, sometimes they want to receive the plans ready to build. That is why we offer home plan modification services. Please see page 189 for specific information on the customizing process and how to get a free quote on the changes you want to make to a home before you buy the plans.

8 order plans

If you've found the home and are ready to order blueprints, we recommend ordering the PDF file format, which offers the most flexibility. A PDF file format will be emailed to you when you order, and it includes a copyright release from the designer, meaning you have the legal right to make changes to the plan if necessary as well as print out as many copies of the plan as you need for building the home one-time. You will be happy to have your blueprints saved electronically so they can easily be shared with your contractor, subcontractors, lender and local building officials. We do, however, offer several different types of plan package depending on your needs, so please refer to page 187 for all plan options available and choose the best one for your particular situation.

Another helpful component in the building process that is available for many of the house plans in this book is a material list. A material list includes not only a detailed list of materials, but it also indicates where various cuts of lumber and other building components are to be used. This will save your general contractor significant time and money since they won't have to create this list before building begins. Visit houseplansandmore.com to see if a material list is available for a home in this book.

9 order materials

You can order materials yourself, or have your contractor do it. Nevertheless, in order to thoroughly enjoy your new home you will want to personally select many of the materials that go into its construction. Today, home improvement stores offer a wide variety of quality building products. Only you can decide what specific types of windows, cabinets, bath fixtures, etc. will make your new home yours. Spend time early on in the construction process looking at the materials and products available.

10 move in

With careful planning and organization, your new home will be built on schedule and ready for your move-in date. Be sure to have all of your important documents in place for the closing of your new home and then you'll be ready to move in and start living your dream.

Browse the pages of Best-Selling House Plans and discover 240 home designs offered in a wide variety of sizes and styles to suit many individuals. From laid-back Craftsman and Country styles, to sleek Modern and classic Traditional, there is a home design here for everyone, and with all of the amenities and features homeowners are looking for in a new home design today. Start your search right now for the perfect home!

Plan #F13-091D-0535

Dimensions:	51' W x 59' D
Heated Sq. Ft.:	3,879
Bedrooms: 4	Bathrooms: 3½
Exterior Walls:	2" x 6"

Foundation: Crawl space standard; slab, basement, daylight basement or walk-out basement for an additional fee

See index for more information

Images provided by designer/architect

Features

- Every so often a home comes around that truly distinguishes itself from the rest, and this is the one
- Step into the warm and inviting foyer and find a functional pocket office to the left
- The formal dining room connects to the kitchen via a stylish butler's pantry
- The vaulted and open kitchen enjoys a huge island that anchors the space and adds casual dining space that overlooks the great room's fireplace
- A sunny breakfast nook enjoys access to the screen porch, which has backyard views and an outdoor fireplace
- All of the bedrooms can be found on the second floor along with an open loft area, and a laundry room
- 2-car front entry garage

First Floor
1,717 sq. ft.

© Copyright by designer/architect

Second Floor
2,162 sq. ft.

Plan #F13-101D-0142

Dimensions:	72' W x 82'6" D
Heated Sq. Ft.:	2,700
Bonus Sq. Ft.:	1,991
Bedrooms: 2	Bathrooms: 2½
Exterior Walls:	2" x 6"
Foundation:	Walk-out basement

See index for more information

Features

- Slightly leaning a bit more toward Modern than Modern Farmhouse, this home does feature the color scheme and details for those who love Modern Farmhouse plans

- The remarkable great room has a towering fireplace, a beamed ceiling and is completely open to the kitchen and dining area

- The luxury master bedroom has covered deck access, a bathroom that feels like a sanctuary, and a dressing room-sized walk-in closet

- The mud room is uncommon in size with tons of storage and cubbies

- The optional lower level has an additional 1,991 square feet of living area and has a rec room with a wet bar, a home theater, two bedrooms, two baths, and a half bath

- 3-car front entry garage

First Floor
2,700 sq. ft.

© Copyright by
designer/architect

Optional
Lower Level
1,991 sq. ft.

Images provided by designer/architect

Plan #F13-155D-0111

Dimensions: 106' W x 110' D
Heated Sq. Ft.: 4,575
Bedrooms: 4   **Bathrooms:** 4½
Foundation: Daylight basement standard; slab or basement for an additional fee

See index for more information

Features

- This one-story luxury home has a Craftsman style exterior that's both rustic and refined
- The kitchen enjoys two islands with one designated for casual dining
- The beautiful beamed ceiling and fireplace add a cozy feel to the great room
- The enormous laundry/hobby room will be a great place to keep everything organized
- A fun game room can be found on the lower level along with bedroom 4, a full bath, and an unfinished basement area
- 3-car front entry garage

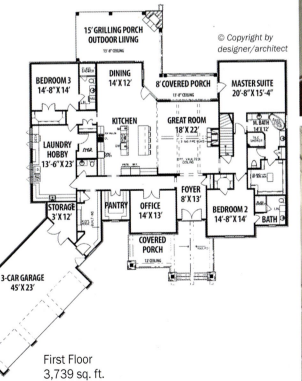

© Copyright by designer/architect

15' GRILLING PORCH OUTDOOR LIIVNG
13'-8" CEILING

BEDROOM 3
14'-8" X 14'

DINING
14' X 12'

8' COVERED PORCH
13'-8" CEILING

MASTER SUITE
20'-8" X 15'-4"

KITCHEN

GREAT ROOM
18' X 22'

M. BATH
14' X 12'

LAUNDRY HOBBY
13'-6" X 23'

FOYER
8' X 13'

STORAGE
3' X 12'

PANTRY

OFFICE
14' X 13'

BEDROOM 2
14'-8" X 14'

BATH

COVERED PORCH
12' CEILING

3-CAR GARAGE
45' X 23'

First Floor
3,739 sq. ft.

Lower Level
836 sq. ft.

COVERED PORCH

BATH

BEDROOM 4

GAME ROOM

UNFINISHED BASEMENT

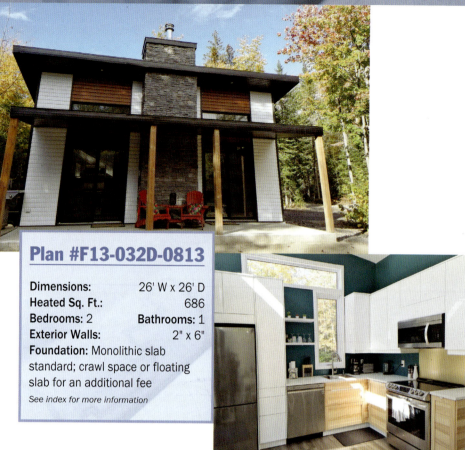

© Copyright by designer/architect

BEDROOM 2
9' 0" x 10' 0"

BEDROOM 1
9' 11" x 10' 0"

KITCHEN/DINING/LIVING
25' 0" x 11' 0"

Plan #F13-032D-0813

Dimensions:	26' W x 26' D
Heated Sq. Ft.:	686
Bedrooms: 2	Bathrooms: 1
Exterior Walls:	2" x 6"

Foundation: Monolithic slab standard; crawl space or floating slab for an additional fee

See index for more information

Images provided by designer/architect

© Copyright by designer/architect

SCREENED GRILLING PORCH
BEADED CEILING
18'-0" X 10'-8"

BREAKFAST ROOM
10'-4" X 10'-6"

MASTER SUITE
13'-6" X 14'-0"
10' BOXED CEILING

GREAT ROOM
17'-2" X 17'-2"
VAULTED CEILING

BEDROOM 3
12'-8" X 11'-0"

KIT.
10'-4" X 11'-6"

M.B.
9'-9" X 10'-4"

BATH

WHP TUB

SHWR

FOYER
12' CEILING

DINING
11'-10" X 12'-0"
10' CEILING

BEDROOM 2
11'-2" X 11'-0"

CLST
13'-6" X 13'-6"

COVERED PORCH
BEADED CEILING

LAU.
6'-0" X 5'-4"

STRG.
4'-8" X 5'-4"

GARAGE
22'-4" X 21'-4"

Images provided by designer/architect

Plan #F13-055D-0988

Dimensions:	57'4" W x 69' D
Heated Sq. Ft.:	2,070
Bonus Sq. Ft.:	332
Bedrooms: 3	Bathrooms: 2½

Foundation: Crawl space or slab standard; basement or daylight basement for an additional fee

See index for more information

First Floor
2,070 sq. ft.

BONUS ROOM
14'-8" X 21'-0"

Optional
Second Floor
332 sq. ft.

Second Floor
294 sq. ft.

Plan #F13-032D-0809

Dimensions: 30' W x 21' D
Heated Sq. Ft.: 924
Bedrooms: 2 **Bathrooms:** 2
Exterior Walls: 2" x 6"
Foundation: Floating slab standard;
crawl space or monolithic slab for
an additional fee

See index for more information

Images provided by designer/architect

First Floor
630 sq. ft.

First Floor
1,845 sq. ft.

Plan #F13-007D-0010

Dimensions: 83' W x 42'4" D
Heated Sq. Ft.: 1,845
Bonus Sq. Ft.: 889
Bedrooms: 3 **Bathrooms:** 2
Foundation: Walk-out basement
standard; crawl space or slab for
an additional fee

See index for more information

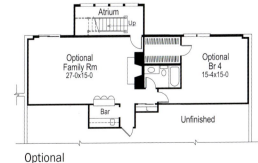

Images provided by designer/architect

Optional
Lower Level
889 sq. ft.

Second Floor
490 sq. ft.

BEDROOM 2
11^2 x 10^6

BEDROOM 3
10^0 x 10^2

BATH 2

LOFT

BALCONY

ATTIC

© Copyright by
designer/architect

WOOD DECK

MASTER BEDROOM
12^8 x 11^{10}

WIC

SHLVS

M. BATH

PANTRY

KITCHEN
18^6 x 19^0

WOOD DECK

LIVING & DINING
14^8 x 19^0

ENTRY

PWDR

STORAGE

CARPORT

PORCH

First Floor
976 sq. ft.

Plan #F13-111D-0037

Dimensions: 28'4" W x 51'8" D
Heated Sq. Ft.: 1,466
Bedrooms: 3 **Bathrooms:** 2½
Foundation: Slab standard; crawl space for an additional fee

See index for more information

Images provided by designer/architect

8 FT DEEP COVERED PORCH

LAUNDRY

CUSTOM SHOWER

HVAC WH

PANTRY

KITCHEN/DINING
19-8 X 13-0

BEDROOM 3
12-0 X 11-6

BATH
8-0 X 9-4

CLO.
8-0x5-6

BATH 2

MASTER BEDROOM
16-0 X 12-6

GREAT ROOM
19-8 X 15-6

BEDROOM 2
12-0 X 11-6

6 FT DEEP COVERED PORCH

© Copyright by
designer/architect

Images provided by designer/architect

Plan #F13-028D-0117

Dimensions: 50' W x 42'6" D
Heated Sq. Ft.: 1,425
Bedrooms: 3 **Bathrooms:** 2
Exterior Walls: 2" x 6"
Foundation: Floating slab standard; monolithic slab, crawl space, basement or walk-out basement for an additional fee

See index for more information

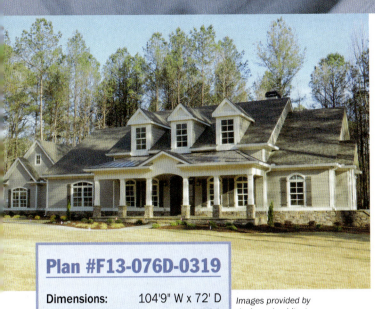

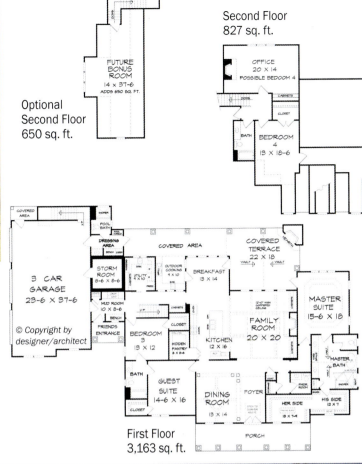

Optional Second Floor
650 sq. ft.

FUTURE BONUS ROOM
14 x 37-6
ADDS 650 SQ. FT.

Second Floor
827 sq. ft.

OFFICE
20 x 14
POSSIBLE BEDROOM 4

BEDROOM 4
13 x 18-6

BATH

© Copyright by designer/architect

First Floor
3,163 sq. ft.

3 CAR GARAGE
23-6 X 37-6

STORM ROOM
8-6 x 8-6

COVERED AREA

COVERED TERRACE
22 x 18

BREAKFAST
13 x 14

OUTDOOR COOKING
4 x 10

FAMILY ROOM
20 x 20

MASTER SUITE
15-6 x 18

BEDROOM 3
13 x 12

KITCHEN
12 x 16

HIDDEN PANTRY
8 x 8-6

MASTER BATH

HIS SIDE
12 x 7

GUEST SUITE
14-6 x 16

BATH

DINING ROOM
13 x 14

FOYER

HER SIDE
13 x 14

PORCH

Plan #F13-076D-0319

Dimensions:	104'9" W x 72' D
Heated Sq. Ft.:	3,990
Bonus Sq. Ft.:	650
Bedrooms: 4	**Bathrooms:** 4½
Foundation:	Slab

See index for more information

Images provided by designer/architect

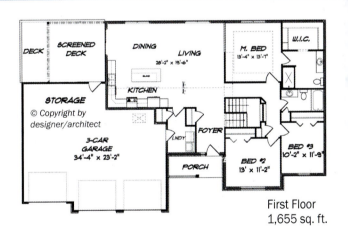

DECK

SCREENED DECK

DINING

LIVING
28'-2" x 19'-6"

M. BED
13'-4" x 13'-1"

W.I.C.

STORAGE

KITCHEN

© Copyright by designer/architect

3-CAR GARAGE
34'-4" x 23'-2"

LNDY

FOYER

PORCH

BED #2
13' x 11'-2"

BED #3
10'-2" x 11'-9"

First Floor
1,655 sq. ft.

BED 4
12' x 11'-4"

FAMILY ROOM
38'-9" x 17'-3"

MECH / STORAGE

FLEX ROOM
14'-6" x 17'

STORAGE

UNEXCAVATED

UNEXCAVATED

Optional Lower Level
1,219 sq. ft.

Plan #F13-159D-0004

Dimensions:	73' W x 44' D
Heated Sq. Ft.:	1,655
Bonus Sq. Ft.:	1,219
Bedrooms: 3	**Bathrooms:** 2
Exterior Walls:	2" x 6"
Foundation:	Walk-out basement

See index for more information

Images provided by designer/architect

Plan #F13-026D-1889

Dimensions:	62' W x 48' D
Heated Sq. Ft.:	1,763
Bedrooms: 3	Bathrooms: 2½

Foundation: Basement standard; crawl space, slab or walk-out basement for an additional fee

See index for more information

Images provided by designer/architect

© Copyright by designer/architect

Mbr.
13⁸ x 14⁰
10'-0" CEILING

Family Room
15⁸ x 20⁰
CATHEDRAL CEILING

Dining Room
10⁰ x 14⁶

ENT

DROP ZONE

DN

Br.2
11⁴ x 12⁰

Br.3
11⁸ x 12⁹
11'-0" CEILING

Garage
31⁴ x 23⁰

Plan #F13-056D-0100

Dimensions:	50' W x 100'9" D
Heated Sq. Ft.:	2,147
Bonus Sq. Ft.:	2,547
Bedrooms: 2	Bathrooms: 2

Foundation: Basement standard; crawl space or slab for an additional fee

See index for more information

Optional Lower Level
2,009 sq. ft.

First Floor
2,147 sq. ft.

Optional Second Floor
538 sq. ft.

© Copyright by designer/architect

Images provided by designer/architect

Plan #F13-026D-2091

Dimensions: 42' W x 51'4" D
Heated Sq. Ft.: 1,603
Bedrooms: 3   **Bathrooms:** 2
Foundation: Basement standard; crawl space, slab or walk-out basement for an additional fee

See index for more information

Images provided by designer/architect

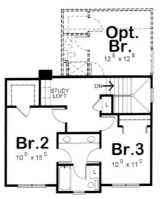

Second Floor
580 sq. ft.

Plan #F13-026D-1876

Dimensions: 46' W x 60' D
Heated Sq. Ft.: 1,995
Bonus Sq. Ft.: 239
Bedrooms: 3   **Bathrooms:** 2½
Foundation: Slab standard; crawl space, basement or walk-out basement for an additional fee

See index for more information

Images provided by designer/architect

First Floor
1,415 sq. ft.

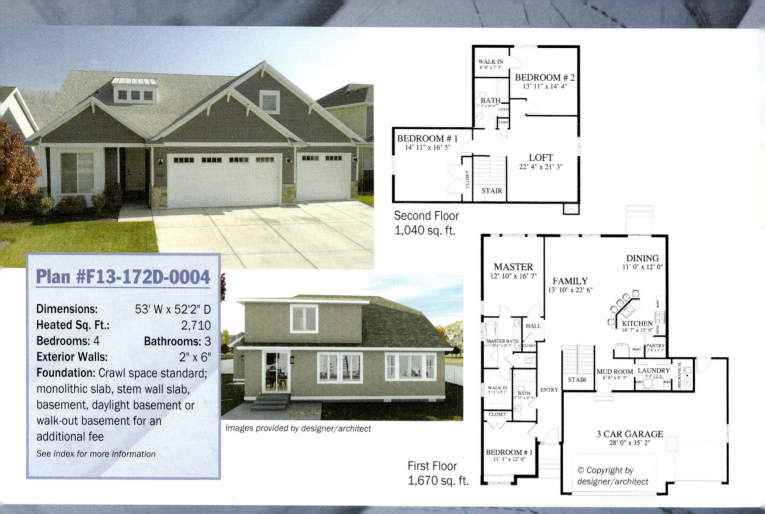

Second Floor
1,040 sq. ft.

WALK IN
6' 0" x 7' 3"

BEDROOM # 2
13' 11" x 14' 4"

BATH

BEDROOM # 1
14' 11" x 16' 3"

LOFT
22' 4" x 21' 3"

CLOSET

STAIR

First Floor
1,670 sq. ft.

MASTER
12' 10" x 16' 7"

FAMILY
13' 10" x 22' 6"

DINING
11' 0" x 12' 0"

HALL

MASTER BATH

KITCHEN
14' 7" x 15' 0"

PANTRY

WALK IN
5' 11" x 4' 3"

BATH

ENTRY

STAIR

MUD ROOM
6' 6" x 8' 3"

LAUNDRY

MECHANICAL

CLOSET

BEDROOM # 1
11' 1" x 12' 6"

3 CAR GARAGE
28' 0" x 35' 2"

© Copyright by
designer/architect

Plan #F13-172D-0004

Dimensions:	53' W x 52'2" D
Heated Sq. Ft.:	2,710
Bedrooms: 4	Bathrooms: 3
Exterior Walls:	2" x 6"

Foundation: Crawl space standard; monolithic slab, stem wall slab, basement, daylight basement or walk-out basement for an additional fee

See index for more information

Images provided by designer/architect

Plan #F13-053D-0002

Dimensions:	56' W x 40' D
Heated Sq. Ft.:	1,668
Bonus Sq. Ft.:	780
Bedrooms: 3	Bathrooms: 2
Foundation:	Basement

See index for more information

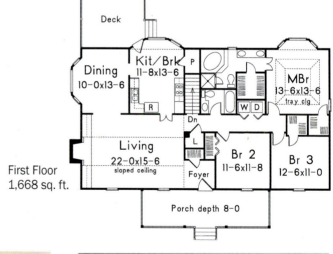

First Floor
1,668 sq. ft.

Deck

Dining
10-0x13-6

Kit/Brk
11-8x13-6

MBr
13-6x13-6
tray clg

Living
22-0x15-6
sloped ceiling

Dn

Br 2
11-6x11-8

Br 3
12-6x11-0

Foyer

Porch depth 8-0

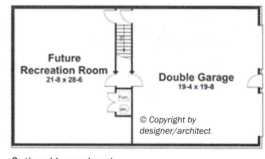

Optional Lower Level
780 sq. ft.

Future
Recreation Room
21-8 x 28-6

Double Garage
19-4 x 19-8

© Copyright by
designer/architect

Images provided by designer/architect

Plan #F13-055D-0342

Dimensions:	60' W x 77'6" D
Heated Sq. Ft.:	2,445
Bonus Sq. Ft.:	758
Bedrooms: 4	Bathrooms: 3½

Foundation: Crawl space or slab standard; basement or daylight basement for an additional fee

See index for more information

Images provided by designer/architect

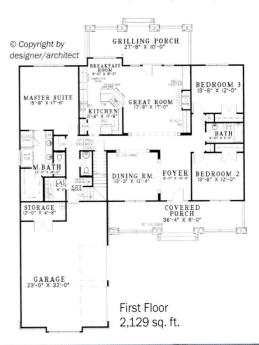

Second Floor
316 sq. ft.

© Copyright by designer/architect

First Floor
2,129 sq. ft.

Images provided by designer/architect

Plan #F13-011D-0013

Dimensions:	60' W x 50' D
Heated Sq. Ft.:	2,001
Bedrooms: 3	Bathrooms: 2
Exterior Walls:	2" x 6"

Foundation: Crawl space or slab standard; basement for an additional fee

See index for more information

Images provided by designer/architect

Plan #F13-149D-0007

Dimensions:	71' W x 48' D
Heated Sq. Ft.:	2,381
Bedrooms: 3	**Bathrooms:** 3½

Foundation: Slab standard; crawl space or basement for an additional fee

See index for more information

Second Floor
827 sq. ft.

© Copyright by designer/architect

First Floor
1,554 sq. ft.

© Copyright by designer/architect

Plan #F13-141D-0061

Dimensions:	46' W x 46' D
Heated Sq. Ft.:	1,273
Bedrooms: 2	**Bathrooms:** 2

Foundation: Crawl space standard; slab, basement or walk-out basement for an additional fee

See index for more information

Images provided by designer/architect

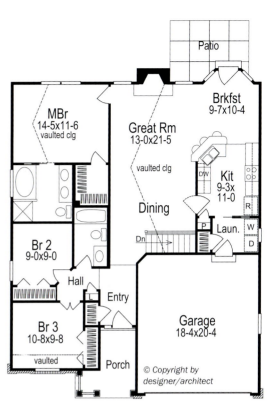

Plan #F13-007D-0060

Dimensions: 38'8" W x 48'4" D
Heated Sq. Ft.: 1,268
Bedrooms: 3 **Bathrooms:** 2
Foundation: Basement standard; crawl space or slab for an additional fee

See index for more information

Images provided by designer/architect

© Copyright by designer/architect

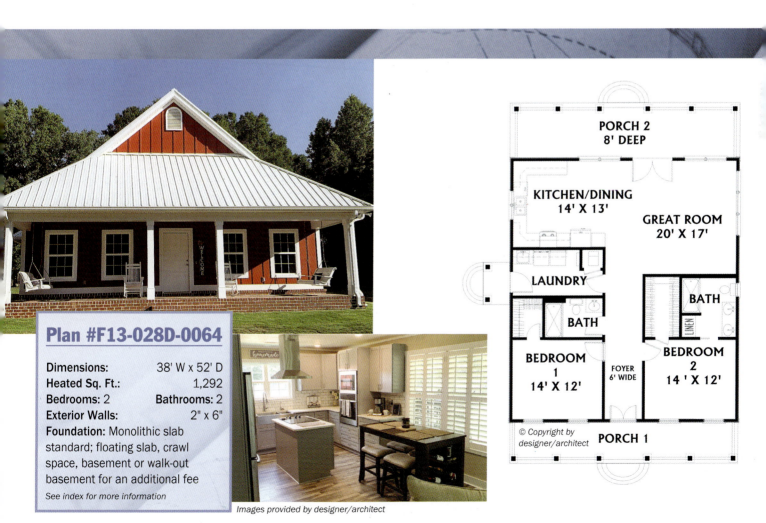

Plan #F13-028D-0064

Dimensions: 38' W x 52' D
Heated Sq. Ft.: 1,292
Bedrooms: 2 **Bathrooms:** 2
Exterior Walls: 2" x 6"
Foundation: Monolithic slab standard; floating slab, crawl space, basement or walk-out basement for an additional fee

See index for more information

Images provided by designer/architect

© Copyright by designer/architect

Plan #F13-170D-0019

Dimensions:	87'2" W x 60'4" D
Heated Sq. Ft.:	2,648
Bedrooms: 4	**Bathrooms:** 2½

Foundation: Slab or monolithic slab, please specify when ordering

See index for more information

Features

- This one-story has a tremendous amount of open space ideal for those who like an airy atmosphere
- There is a formal dining room as well as a casual eating area off the kitchen
- A large kitchen island overlooks the family room and its centered fireplace
- A small office is right around the corner from the kitchen in a secluded hallway
- The master bedroom enjoys its privacy, a large bath with both a shower and a spa style tub, and a large walk-in closet
- 3-car side entry garage

© Copyright by designer/architect

Images provided by designer/architect

Plan #F13-091D-0509

Dimensions:	72' W x 69'2" D
Heated Sq. Ft.:	2,886
Bonus Sq. Ft.:	270
Bedrooms: 4	**Bathrooms:** 4½
Exterior Walls:	2" x 6"

Foundation: Crawl space standard; slab, basement, daylight basement or walk-out basement for an additional fee

See index for more information

Features

- Simply stunning Modern Farmhouse includes many extras on every homeowner's wish list including an office and a mud room
- The kitchen features a walk-in pantry with a barn style door, a huge island and dining space
- The luxury master bedroom has a dressing room style walk-in closet and a spa style bath
- The mud room is accessed from a handy side entrance as well as the garage
- The second floor has three bedrooms and a open loft space, ideal as a teen hang-out spot
- The garage has an overhead door that can be raised on the pool and patio side where outdoor living space can be created in a shady spot that's also convenient to a pool bath
- The future bonus space on the second floor has an additional 270 square feet of living area
- 3-car side entry garage

First Floor
1,800 sq. ft.

Second Floor
1,086 sq. ft.

Images provided by designer/architect

© Copyright by designer/architect

Plan #F13-101D-0126

Dimensions:	102'3" W x 63' D
Heated Sq. Ft.:	3,907
Bonus Sq. Ft.:	2,052
Bedrooms: 4	**Bathrooms:** 3½
Exterior Walls:	2" x 6"

Foundation: Basement, daylight basement or walk-out basement, please specify when ordering

See index for more information

Features

- The open kitchen with a huge island enjoys views of the vaulted living room and sunny dining area
- Behind the kitchen is a huge laundry room, a mud room, and a walk-in pantry
- The private master bedroom has a cozy corner fireplace, sliding glass doors to a deck, and a bath with a walk-in closet
- The second floor has three large additional bedrooms, and a loft
- The optional lower level has an additional 2,052 square feet of living area including a rec room, a movie room, a workout room, an office, a bedroom, and a bath
- 3-car side entry garage

Second Floor
1,322 sq. ft.

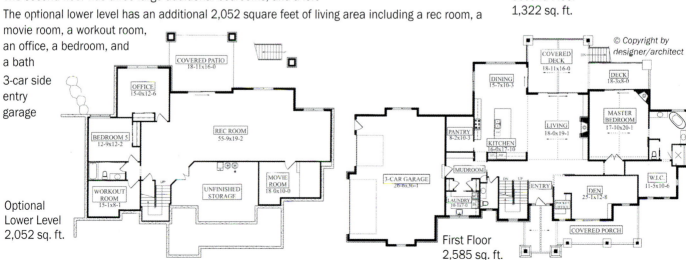

© Copyright by designer/architect

Optional Lower Level 2,052 sq. ft.

First Floor 2,585 sq. ft.

Plan #F13-123D-0056

Dimensions:	55' W x 55' D
Heated Sq. Ft.:	1,701
Bedrooms: 3	**Bathrooms:** 2

Foundation: Basement standard; crawl space, slab or walk-out basement for an additional fee

See index for more information

Images provided by designer/architect

Features

- A perfect split bedroom ranch home designed with today's popular Modern Farmhouse design in mind

- The great room is topped with a 10' ceiling and enjoys views of the dining area and kitchen featuring a large island

- The private master bedroom has its own private bath and a walk-in closet

- Enter the mud room from the garage and drop belongings here to keep them out of the main gathering spaces

- The large covered front porch is an inviting way to relax and enjoy the outdoors in the shade

- 3-car front entry garage

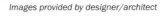

© Copyright by designer/architect

Br.2 10 x 11

Grt. Rm. 18 x 16 10'-0" Ceiling

Din. 12 x 10

Mbr. 12 x 14 10'-0" Ceiling

K. 12 x 11

Built-In

Lin.

Br.3 10 x 11

DN

Pantry

R

Mud Room

D W

Catch-All

Bench/ Lockers

Covered Porch

Gar. 33 x 22

Plan #F13-101D-0149

Dimensions:	74'6" W x 65'6" D
Heated Sq. Ft.:	2,105
Bonus Sq. Ft.:	1,872
Bedrooms: 2	Bathrooms: 2½
Exterior Walls:	2" x 6"
Foundation:	Basement

See index for more information

Images provided by designer/architect

Features

- This stunning home has a simple floor plan that's open and airy the moment you walk in
- One of the main attractions in this home design is the huge mud/laundry room that is filled with tons of storage space
- The great room has sliding glass doors leading to a rear wrap-around covered patio
- The master bedroom has its own patio, a walk-in closet, and a large bath with a unique shower/free-standing tub room
- The optional lower level has an additional 1,872 square feet of living area that includes a rec room, two bedrooms, two full baths, and a gym
- 3-car side entry garage

First Floor
2,105 sq. ft.

© Copyright by designer/architect

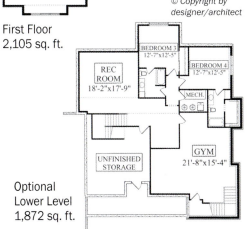

Optional
Lower Level
1,872 sq. ft.

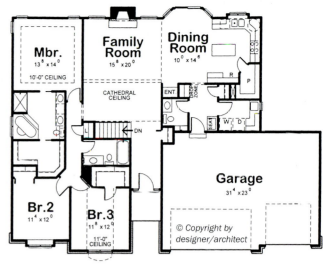

Plan #F13-026D-1722

Images provided by designer/architect

Dimensions: 62' W x 48' D
Heated Sq. Ft.: 1,763
Bedrooms: 3 **Bathrooms:** 2½
Foundation: Basement standard; crawl space, slab or walk-out basement for an additional fee

See index for more information

Plan #F13-060D-0251

Images provided by designer/architect

Dimensions: 47'2" W x 70' D
Heated Sq. Ft.: 2,106
Bonus Sq. Ft.: 436
Bedrooms: 3 **Bathrooms:** 2½
Foundation: Slab

See index for more information

Second Floor
99 sq. ft.

First Floor
2,007 sq. ft.

Second Floor
1,184 sq. ft.

First Floor
1,289 sq. ft.

© Copyright by
designer/architect

**Optional
Lower Level**
1,350 sq. ft.

Plan #F13-172D-0032

Dimensions:	49' W x 42'6" D
Heated Sq. Ft.:	2,473
Bonus Sq. Ft.:	1,350
Bedrooms: 4	**Bathrooms: 2½**
Exterior Walls:	2" x 6"

Foundation: Basement standard; monolithic slab, stem wall slab, crawl space, daylight basement or walk-out basement for an additional fee

See index for more information

Images provided by designer/architect

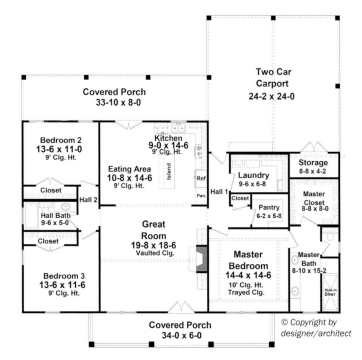

Images provided by designer/architect

© Copyright by designer/architect

Plan #F13-077D-0293

Dimensions:	58' W x 58'6" D
Heated Sq. Ft.:	1,800
Bedrooms: 3	**Bathrooms: 2**

Foundation: Crawl space or slab, please specify when ordering

See index for more information

© Copyright by designer/architect

First Floor
3,424 sq. ft.

Master Bedroom 15⁴ · 17¹⁰
Covered Patio
Family Room 16⁹ · 19²
Bedroom 5 12⁰ · 11⁰
w.i.c.
w.i.c.
Living Rm. 15⁰ · 17²
Nook 11⁸ · 10⁰
Bedroom 4 12⁰ · 12⁰
Kitchen 18⁰ · 13¹⁰
Bedroom 3 13⁸ · 12⁰
Mstr. Bath
pan.
Foyer
Dining Rm. 13⁰ · 13⁰
Laundry
Bedroom 2 11⁸ · 15⁰
Entry
3 Car Garage 22⁶ · 35⁰

Game Room 15⁴ · 26⁰
w.i.c.

Optional Second Floor
507 sq. ft.

Plan #F13-047D-0056

Dimensions:	82'4" W x 83'8" D
Heated Sq. Ft.:	3,424
Bonus Sq. Ft.:	507
Bedrooms: 5	**Bathrooms:** 4
Exterior Walls:	Concrete block
Foundation:	Slab

See index for more information

Images provided by designer/architect

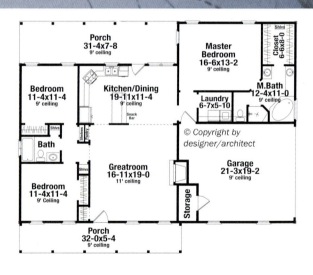

Porch 31-4x7-8 9' ceiling
Master Bedroom 16-6x13-2 9' ceiling
Closet 6-6x8-0
Bedroom 11-4x11-4 9' ceiling
Kitchen/Dining 19-11x11-4 9' ceiling
M.Bath 12-4x11-0 9' ceiling
Laundry 6-7x5-10
Snack Bar
Bath
© Copyright by designer/architect
Bedroom 11-4x11-4 9' Ceiling
Greatroom 16-11x19-0 11' ceiling
Garage 21-3x19-2 9' ceiling
Storage
Porch 32-0x5-4 9' ceiling

Plan #F13-084D-0016

Dimensions:	56' W x 45'8" D
Heated Sq. Ft.:	1,492
Bedrooms: 3	**Bathrooms:** 2

Foundation: Slab standard; crawl space or basement for an additional fee

See index for more information

Images provided by designer/architect

Second Floor
1,108 sq. ft.

Mstr. Bdrm.
16-0X15-6

Vault'd Ceiling

Master Bath

W.I.C

Lndry

Bdrm #2
10-10X11-5

Bdrm #3
10-10X13-4

Bdrm #4
12 10X12-0

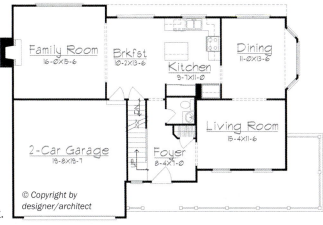

Family Room
16-0X15-6

Brkfst
10-2X13-6

Kitchen
9-7X11-0

Dining
11-0X13-6

Living Room
15-4X11-6

2-Car Garage
19-8X19-7

Foyer
8-4X7-0

© Copyright by
designer/architect

First Floor
1,027 sq. ft.

Plan #F13-027D-0005

Dimensions:	48' W x 34' D
Heated Sq. Ft.:	2,135
Bedrooms: 4	**Bathrooms:** 2½
Foundation: Basement standard; slab for an additional fee	

See index for more information

Images provided by designer/architect

Plan #F13-101D-0047

Dimensions:	99' W x 81' D
Heated Sq. Ft.:	2,478
Bonus Sq. Ft.:	1,795
Bedrooms: 2	**Bathrooms:** 2½
Exterior Walls:	2" x 6"
Foundation:	Walk-out basement

See index for more information

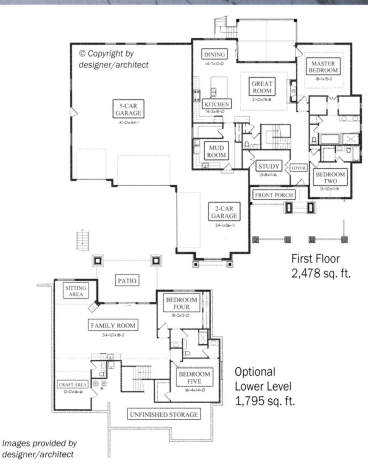

© Copyright by
designer/architect

5-CAR GARAGE
41-0x44-1

DINING
14-7x12-0

GREAT ROOM
21-0x19-8

KITCHEN
14-3x16-0

MUD ROOM

STUDY
13-8x11-6

FOYER

MASTER BEDROOM
18-1x15-2

BEDROOM TWO
13-10x11-5

FRONT PORCH

2-CAR GARAGE
24-1x26-11

First Floor
2,478 sq. ft.

SITTING AREA

PATIO

FAMILY ROOM
34-10x18-2

CRAFT AREA
12-0x16-0

BEDROOM FOUR
15-2x12-0

BEDROOM FIVE
16-4x14-0

UNFINISHED STORAGE

Optional Lower Level
1,795 sq. ft.

Images provided by designer/architect

Plan #F13-026D-1977

Dimensions:	44' W x 54' D
Heated Sq. Ft.:	2,232
Bonus Sq. Ft.:	240
Bedrooms: 4	**Bathrooms:** 3
Exterior Walls:	2" x 6"

Foundation: Basement standard; crawl space, slab or walk-out basement for an additional fee

See index for more information

Images provided by designer/architect

Second Floor
556 sq. ft.

First Floor
1,676 sq. ft.

© Copyright by designer/architect

Plan #F13-027D-0007

Dimensions:	64' W x 48' D
Heated Sq. Ft.:	2,422
Bedrooms: 3	**Bathrooms:** 2½
Foundation:	Basement

See index for more information

Images provided by designer/architect

Second Floor
734 sq. ft.

First Floor
1,688 sq. ft.

© Copyright by designer/architect

Plan #F13-026D-2017

Dimensions:	50' W x 58' D
Heated Sq. Ft.:	1,676
Bedrooms: 3	**Bathrooms:** 2

Foundation: Basement standard; crawl space, slab or walk-out basement for an additional fee

See index for more information

Images provided by designer/architect

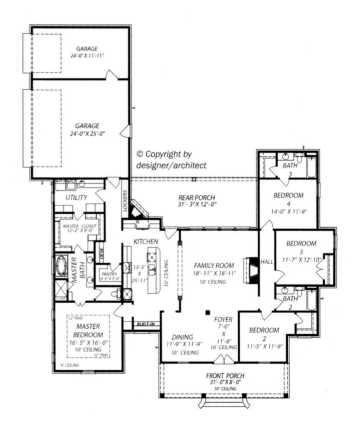

Plan #F13-170D-0012

Dimensions:	74'8" W x 87'7" D
Heated Sq. Ft.:	2,605
Bedrooms: 4	**Bathrooms:** 3
Exterior Walls:	2" x 6"

Foundation: Monolithic slab or slab standard; crawl space, basement or daylight basement for an additional fee

See index for more information

Images provided by designer/architect

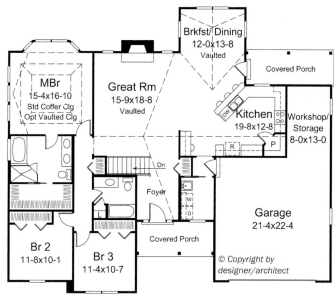

Plan #F13-121D-0036

Dimensions: 60'4" W x 52' D
Heated Sq. Ft.: 1,820
Bedrooms: 3   **Bathrooms:** 2
Foundation: Basement standard; crawl space or slab for an additional fee

See index for more information

Images provided by designer/architect

© Copyright by designer/architect

Plan #F13-032D-1112

Dimensions: 66'4" W x 35'4" D
Heated Sq. Ft.: 2,380
Bonus Sq. Ft.: 1,280
Bedrooms: 4   **Bathrooms:** 2½
Exterior Walls: 2" x 6"
Foundation: Basement standard; crawl space, monolithic slab or floating slab for an additional fee

See index for more information

Second Floor 1,100 sq. ft.

First Floor 1,280 sq. ft.

Optional Lower Level 1,280 sq. ft.

© Copyright by designer/architect

Images provided by designer/architect

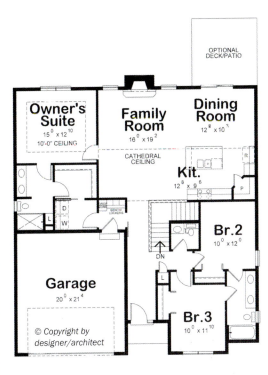

Plan #F13-026D-2143

Dimensions: 45' W x 47'8" D
Heated Sq. Ft.: 1,642
Bedrooms: 3   **Bathrooms:** 2½
Exterior Walls: 2" x 6"
Foundation: Basement standard; crawl space, slab or walk-out basement for an additional fee

See index for more information

Images provided by designer/architect

Plan #F13-007D-0055

Images provided by designer/architect

Dimensions: 67' W x 51'4" D
Heated Sq. Ft.: 2,029
Bedrooms: 3   **Bathrooms:** 2
Foundation: Basement standard; crawl space or slab for an additional fee

See index for more information

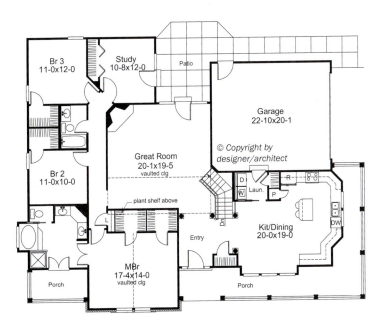

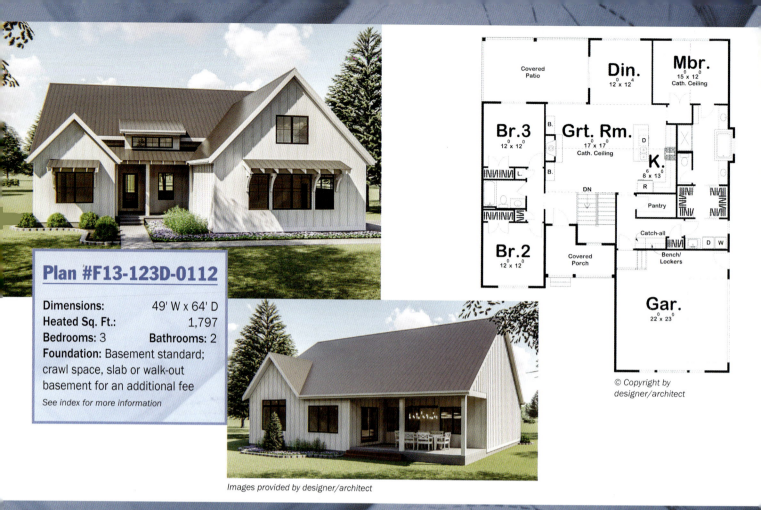

Plan #F13-123D-0112

Dimensions: 49' W x 64' D
Heated Sq. Ft.: 1,797
Bedrooms: 3   Bathrooms: 2
Foundation: Basement standard; crawl space, slab or walk-out basement for an additional fee

See index for more information

Images provided by designer/architect

© Copyright by designer/architect

Plan #F13-011D-0697

Dimensions: 27'6" W x 38' D
Heated Sq. Ft.: 1,619
Bedrooms: 3   Bathrooms: 2½
Exterior Walls: 2" x 6"
Foundation: Crawl space or slab standard; basement for an additional fee

See index for more information

Second Floor
784 sq. ft.

First Floor
835 sq. ft.

© Copyright by designer/architect

Images provided by designer/architect

© Copyright by designer/architect

Plan #F13-155D-0052

Dimensions: 60'10" W x 78' D
Heated Sq. Ft.: 4,072
Bedrooms: 3   **Bathrooms:** 3½
Foundation: Crawl space or slab, please specify when ordering
See index for more information

Images provided by designer/architect

Second Floor
1,402 sq. ft.

First Floor
2,670 sq. ft.

Plan #F13-077D-0302

Dimensions: 57'4" W x 72' D
Heated Sq. Ft.: 1,812
Bedrooms: 3   **Bathrooms:** 2½
Foundation: Crawl space or slab, please specify when ordering
See index for more information

Images provided by designer/architect

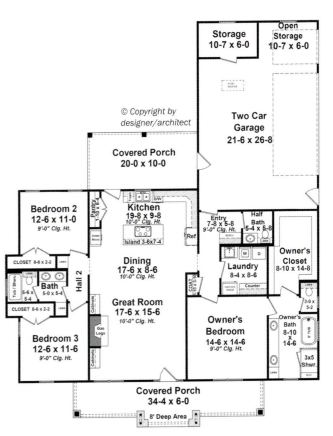

© Copyright by designer/architect

Plan #F13-011D-0684

Dimensions:	40' W x 59' D
Heated Sq. Ft.:	1,373
Bedrooms: 3	**Bathrooms:** 2
Exterior Walls:	2" x 6"

Foundation: Crawl space or slab standard; basement for an additional fee

See index for more information

Features

- A compact, yet stylish Modern Farmhouse design is just the right size for the empty nester, or the first-time home buyer
- The split bedroom floor plan ensures privacy for the homeowners and guests
- The vaulted great room has wonderful covered porch views through a trio of large windows
- The kitchen enjoys an island with sink, and a pantry with washer and dryer space behind a pocket door
- Two secondary bedrooms share a full bath near the front of the home to complete the design
- 2-car front entry garage

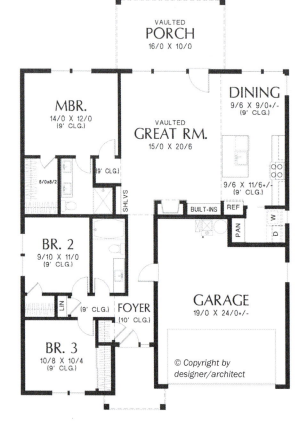

Images provided by designer/architect

Plan #F13-123D-0146

Dimensions:	66' W x 62' D
Heated Sq. Ft.:	2,309
Bonus Sq. Ft.:	1,706
Bedrooms: 4	Bathrooms: 3½

Foundation: Basement standard; crawl space, slab or walk-out basement for an additional fee

See index for more information

Images provided by designer/architect

Features

- A huge covered front porch and a covered patio create outdoor living areas that are seamless to the interior
- The mud room by the garage entrance is accompanied by a roomy laundry room, a half bath and a bench with lockers above
- The great room is topped with a cathedral ceiling that opens up the interior tremendously
- The optional lower level has an additional 1,244 square feet of living area and features a family room with bar and a great home theater; while the optional second floor has an additional 462 square feet of living area
- 2-car side entry garage

Optional Second Floor 462 sq. ft.

© Copyright by designer/architect

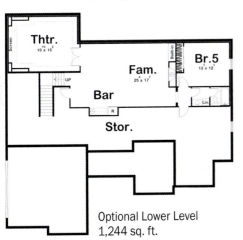

Optional Lower Level 1,244 sq. ft.

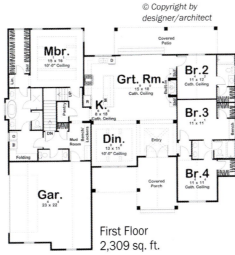

First Floor 2,309 sq. ft.

the wow factor:
The "It" Features
home buyers want

The features found in homes today are there for a reason; these are the things homeowners are asking for to make their lives easier! Home buyers' attitudes have shifted and today's homeowners are practical and mindful. They are content with a smaller home featuring an open floor plan, which typically requires less maintenance. They ideally want to build with affordable and sustainable materials. Their need for the bells and whistles has waned, and they seek a modern, less cluttered style overall, but since the pandemic personal touches that make it feel comforting and more personal have become a priority to many. Homes of yesteryear can't compete with the amazing new home designs that incorporate so many automated features and great open floor plans. Let's take a closer look at several of the in-demand features sought in new homes today.

Unless noted, copyright by designer/architect; Page 40, top: Plan #101D-0127; bottom: Plan #101D-0121; Page 41, top, left: Plan #011S-0196, Bob Greenspan, photographer; top, right: Plan #161D-0001; bottom: Plan #011S-0192. See additional photos and purchase plans at houseplansandmore.com.

go with the flow

Today's floor plans have less square footage, so they must maximize every last square foot to the fullest. Homes designed today have fewer rooms, so rooms have to serve many purposes. Open floor plans still remain most popular and offer the potential for a smaller home to feel large and functional. However, since the pandemic, the need for more compartmentalized spaces has increased slightly with many family members working and learning from home. So, the seamless flow from the dining area, kitchen, and living area seen with an open floor plan has created some issues with functionality for some families. Some homeowners are looking for "flex" spaces that can convert on the fly and offer alternative solutions for work, learning or play. But, it's safe to say that all homeowners still want the interior to flow freely to the outdoor area. Similar flooring color and furniture outdoors tends to visually extend the home even farther making a smaller home feel comfortably roomy and less confined. Homeowners desire outdoor spaces that mimic their home's interior and include a dedicated area for sitting and dining space. Many of these spaces include outdoor fireplaces, or a calming water element. Before the pandemic homeowners were looking for less yard space; just enough to have an oasis to retreat to, but not enough to create additional chores and maintenance, but, many homeowners since the pandemic have moved out of more densely populated suburban areas and are seeking more yard space.

An open flow is even more important than size. So more windows and doors, and fewer walls are optimal features that add a feeling of spaciousness and volume. Formal dining and living rooms are considered spaces of the past, and in their place are flex spaces that can be converted to home offices, a guest room, or a kid's playroom or home school space. With today's family, flexibility is key. High ceilings throughout are more popular now than attention-seeking dramatic two-story foyers or decorative ceiling in only certain rooms.

clean living

With open, airy spaces also comes the desire for sleek interior spaces and furnishings especially in the kitchen where clutter can easily occur. Architecturally, today's homes are using simpler lines. Think less trim work and fancy crown moldings, and more streamline Craftsman and Prairie style woodwork and rustic beams. Cabinet styles are less ornate and Traditional now, and sleek Modern cabinets are popular. Many kitchens are ditching cabinet hardware entirely.

Quartz countertops are being chosen more often than granite since they have more subtle surfaces with less pattern. Wide plank style flooring is still the most popular, but the dark colors have been toned down to more natural, raw wood tones. With sleek cabinets and counters, homeowners love the look of matte appliances rather than the shiny steel counterparts. Definitely a more subdued look, these appliances tend to hide scratches and fingerprints much better.

i am an island

Kitchen islands are a must-have since they offer additional prep space, storage, casual dining space, and are steps from the dining area. Open shelving in a kitchen can offer an open feel and easy access for frequently used items. Pantry sizes have also increased, while the amount of cabinets have decreased. This gives the illusion of a sleeker kitchen overall.

Kitchens have become larger and more open with less clutter, with most appliances hidden in the pantry. Basically, today's best features in the kitchen are popular because they make a kitchen appear simple, clean and uncluttered.

peace out

Sleek, clean living continues into the bathroom, too. No longer are homeowners requesting large garden style tubs that often featured multiple steps and ornate columns. Oversized garden tubs simply take up too much bathroom real estate in today's smaller homes. Instead, low-curb or open walk-in showers often with practically invisible glass surrounds are trending. If the home is larger and there is space for a tub, then homeowners are requesting free-standing modern style tubs. Large floor tiles and sleek fixtures complement this Zen-like space to create a feeling of complete and total tranquility.

lite brite

White is still popular for both kitchen and baths, but layered looks that add light paint colors, raw wood tones, and mixed cabinets or island colors are gaining popularity. Shades of green and blue are quite popular, but gray and black are also making a comeback. Oversized windows, glass doors and skylights also help carry out the light and bright theme to the fullest. Many new homes are being painted a color, called, "greige," which is a hybrid of beige and gray, but sage green and gray-blue are now popular, too. These subtle colors from nature have made their way into the lineup along with the classic gray-beige neutrals of the past few years. Unique backsplash tile is being arranged in interesting, artistic ways. Minimalism has been replaced in some respects by maximalism thanks to homeowners' desires for bold statement lighting, unique tile, and even whimsical nature-inspired wallpaper prints and patterns.

go green

Homeowners today are interested in value, environmentally sound material choices, and products that will provide lasting durability and comfort. Those building a new home realize that it's worth paying a little more for certain materials because it will result in bigger savings over the lifespan of the home. From low-E windows to high efficiency air conditioners, there are countless ways to include green building materials, and all provide an opportunity to save money on your utility bills.

Home buyers are also more interested than ever in maintaining good indoor air quality. So, green products that use zero VOCs or low VOCs are extremely popular. Practically every item in your home emits chemicals into the air. From paint and varnishes to carpeting fibers and drapery textiles, all of these things fill the air with allergens that can be harmful. Green products typically contain chemicals less harsh to our environment and offer a gentler solution overall.

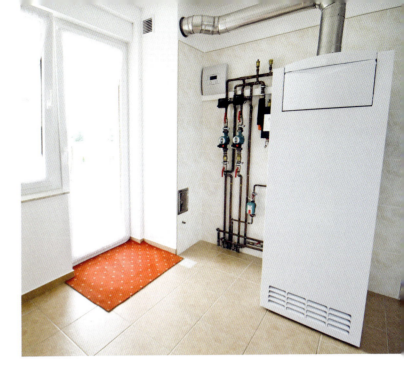

smart solutions

The fastest growing trend in home design is automation. In the last few years and since the creation of smart phones, the number of products available to automate your home has flooded the market. Products that act as a "hub" can be activated with the touch of a button, and they can control and manage multiple apps devoted to maintaining your home. From monitoring your home's security, efficiency, comfort level, and inhabitants, you can virtually manage your home and everything in it all with the touch of your fingertip on your smart phone. Home buyers are also seeking more electrical outlets throughout a home in addition to high quality Wi-Fi access for every room. And, builders are hearing frequent requests for docking stations, or car charging stations in garages as the popularity of electronic cars continues to grow.

just drop it

Also, in line with making life easier is the popular feature of a drop zone. A drop zone is typically an area near the garage entrance that features lockers, cubbies, a bench, and possibly a desk with a charging station for hand held devices and smart phones. It's another practical and smart storage solution homeowners are deeming a necessity especially with families.

we are family

Our pets are becoming more a part of the family than ever before and it's dictating the types of features being seen integrated into home design. Built-in bowls, crates, gates, and beds make a home feel like all attention to detail was considered throughout the design process instead of these necessities appearing like an after-thought for the furry family member.

Thoughtful, practical, and purposeful. Today's homeowners are a unique group who want a home to feel like it was entirely designed for them. Everything in it should serve a purpose, while offering ease with life's everyday challenges for every person who dwells there right down to the family pet.

Unless noted, copyright by designer/architect; Page 46, top, left clockwise: The ultimate luxury drop zone, Erin Crain Interiors, erincrain.com, Bernard Andre, photographer; Laundry room drop zone combo, Plan #F13-091D-0534 on page 101; ClosetMaid® Built-in drop zone center, Plan #101D-0107, Robert Yone, photographer; ClosetMaid® keeps things organized in the perfect drawer organizer—even better include power supply for charging your devices, closetmaid.com; Unitek Y-2172 [PowerPort 96W/2.4A Max] 10-Port USB Charger Charging Station for multiple devices, amazon.com; The ultimate planning center and drop zone with work space, Plan #011S-0189; Page 47, top, left: Laundry and luxury dog room combo, nextluxury.com; middle, top to bottom: Built-in dog gate, madebymood.com, Jordan Powers; Built-in dog bowl, subzero-wolf.com; Clever feline space, Erin Crain Interiors, erincrain.com, Bernard Andre, photographer; right, top to bottom: Three's company!—more great dog spaces, nextluxury.com; Terracotta Design Build Company's custom dog space solutions, terracottadesignbuild.com; Built-in cage and dog bed, maisonderevebuilders.com; See additional photos and purchase plans at houseplansandmore.com.

Plan #F13-084D-0093

Dimensions: 72'10" W x 69'8" D
Heated Sq. Ft.: 2,480
Bonus Sq. Ft.: 1,957
Bedrooms: 4   **Bathrooms:** 2
Foundation: Slab standard; crawl space or basement for an additional fee

See index for more information

Features

- Enjoy relaxed Modern Farmhouse living in this one-story design with plenty of second floor bonus space
- The open living area with fireplace and tray ceiling flow into the dining area and beyond to the kitchen
- Off the garage is a mud room, step-in pantry, and a separate laundry room, which are all conveniently around the corner from the kitchen
- The optional second floor has an additional 1,957 square feet of living area
- 2-car side entry garage

Images provided by designer/architect

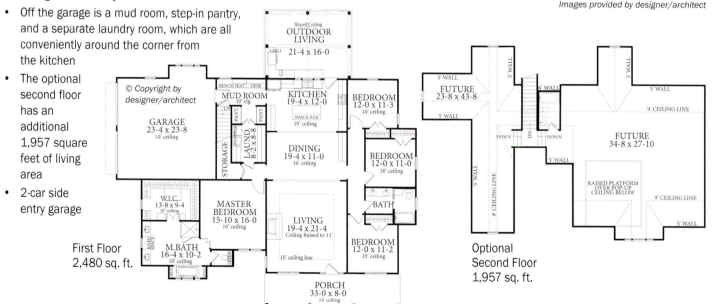

First Floor
2,480 sq. ft.

Optional
Second Floor
1,957 sq. ft.

Plan #F13-019D-0046

Dimensions: 125'5" W x 76'1" D
Heated Sq. Ft.: 2,413
Bedrooms: 3 **Bathrooms:** 2½
Foundation: Slab standard; crawl space or basement for an additional fee

See index for more information

Features

- This stunning Southwestern inspired home combines stone and stucco to create a home with tons of style and curb appeal
- The courtyard front entry offers a private escape for enjoying morning coffee or a cocktail at happy hour
- The grand great room is the main focal point as you enter the home thanks to its centered fireplace and tall ceilings with beams
- Off the kitchen is a handy flex room that could become a great home office, formal dining room or kid's play space
- The private master bedroom offers a luxurious environment for relaxing at the end of the day
- 3-car rear entry garage

Images provided by designer/architect

© Copyright by designer/architect

Plan #F13-123D-0258

Dimensions:	62' W x 38' D
Heated Sq. Ft.:	1,695
Bedrooms: 3	Bathrooms: 2
Exterior Walls:	2" x 6"

Foundation: Slab standard; crawl space, basement or walk-out basement for an additional fee

See index for more information

Features

- Casual country living has never been easier than it is with this simple one-story open floor plan with a spacious cathedral ceiling
- The L-shaped kitchen opens to the family room with fireplace and dining area
- The master bedroom resides on the left of the home and features a 11' tray ceiling, a private bath with a double bowl vanity, a separate shower, and a large walk-in shower
- Two additional bedrooms can be found on the right side of the home and share a nearby bath

Images provided by designer/architect

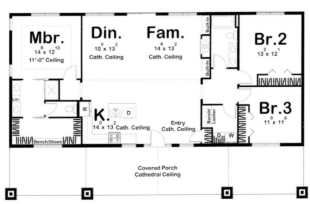

© Copyright by designer/architect

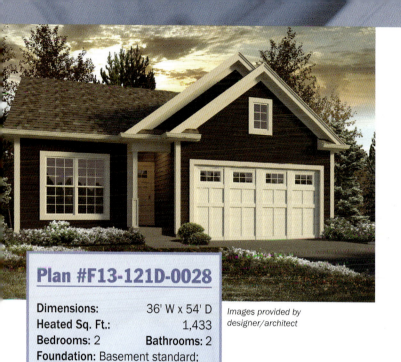

Images provided by designer/architect

Plan #F13-121D-0028

Dimensions: 36' W x 54' D
Heated Sq. Ft.: 1,433
Bedrooms: 2   **Bathrooms:** 2
Foundation: Basement standard; crawl space or slab for an additional fee

See index for more information

Patio

Kit
10-4x11-8
Vaulted

Dining
10-4x11-8
Vaulted

MBr
14-0x16-0
Vaulted
Opt Coffer

Great Rm
17-8x16-3
Vaulted

Plant Shelf
Above

Dn

Entry

Br 2
11-4x10-0

Garage
19-4x21-0

Porch

© Copyright by designer/architect

Plan #F13-091D-0536

Dimensions: 40' W x 60'6" D
Heated Sq. Ft.: 2,889
Bedrooms: 4   **Bathrooms:** 3½
Exterior Walls: 2" x 6"
Foundation: Crawl space standard; slab for an additional fee

See index for more information

Images provided by designer/architect

Second Floor
1,328 sq. ft.

BEDROOM
12 x 12-2
8' clg.

wic

bath

BEDROOM
11 x 11-6
8' clg.

lin

w/d

bath

wic

LOFT
17 x 17-6
8' clg.

dn

wic

BEDROOM
11 x 12
8' clg.

© Copyright by designer/architect

First Floor
1,561 sq. ft.

COVERED PORCH
8-6 x 15
128 sq. ft.

9' clg.

DINETTE
11 x 12

MASTER SUITE
12-6 x 14
9' clg.

9' clg.

GREAT ROOM
14 x 17

KITCHEN
11 x 15-2

fp

M. BATH
9' clg.

wine bar

pan.

WIC
5-6 x 12-6
9' clg.

up

MUD/ LAUND.

w

2-CAR GAR.
21 x 22

447 sq. ft.

OFFICE/ DEN
11 x 12-6
9' clg.

FOY.

FRONT PORCH
6 x 19

Plan #F13-144D-0023

Dimensions:	58' W x 32' D
Heated Sq. Ft.:	928
Bedrooms: 2	**Bathrooms:** 2
Exterior Walls:	2" x 6"

Foundation: Crawl space or slab, please specify when ordering

See index for more information

Images provided by designer/architect

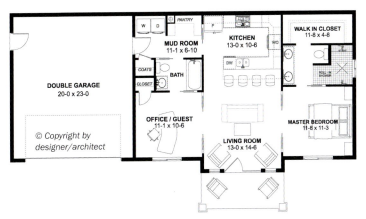

© Copyright by designer/architect

Plan #F13-032D-1152

Dimensions:	46' W x 32' D
Heated Sq. Ft.:	1,912
Bonus Sq. Ft.:	952
Bedrooms: 3	**Bathrooms:** 2½
Exterior Walls:	2" x 6"

Foundation: Basement standard; crawl space, monolithic slab or floating slab for an additional fee

See index for more information

Images provided by designer/architect

Second Floor
960 sq. ft.

First Floor
952 sq. ft.

Optional
Lower Level
952 sq. ft.

© Copyright by designer/architect

Plan #F13-163D-0016

Dimensions: 60'4" W x 64' D
Heated Sq. Ft.: 1,825
Bedrooms: 3   **Bathrooms:** 3
Exterior Walls: 2" x 6"
Foundation: Crawl space

See index for more information

Images provided by designer/architect

Second Floor
753 sq. ft.

First Floor
1,072 sq. ft.

© Copyright by designer/architect

Plan #F13-011D-0687

Dimensions: 74' W x 55' D
Heated Sq. Ft.: 1,975
Bedrooms: 4   **Bathrooms:** 2
Exterior Walls: 2" x 6"
Foundation: Crawl space or slab
standard; basement for an
additional fee

See index for more information

Images provided by designer/architect

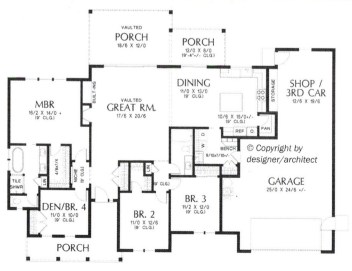

© Copyright by designer/architect

First Floor
3,204 sq. ft.

© Copyright by designer/architect

Images provided by designer/architect

Plan #F13-076D-0281

Dimensions: 103'5" W x 100'10" D
Heated Sq. Ft.: 3,204
Bonus Sq. Ft.: 3,596
Bedrooms: 4 **Bathrooms:** 3½
Foundation: Basement

See index for more information

Optional
Lower Level
3,596 sq. ft.

Images provided by designer/architect

© Copyright by designer/architect

Plan #F13-111D-0081

Dimensions: 54'6" W x 54'9" D
Heated Sq. Ft.: 2,137
Bonus Sq. Ft.: 247
Bedrooms: 3 **Bathrooms:** 2
Foundation: Slab standard; crawl space for an additional fee

See index for more information

Optional
Second Floor
247 sq. ft.

Detached
Garage

First Floor
2,137 sq. ft.

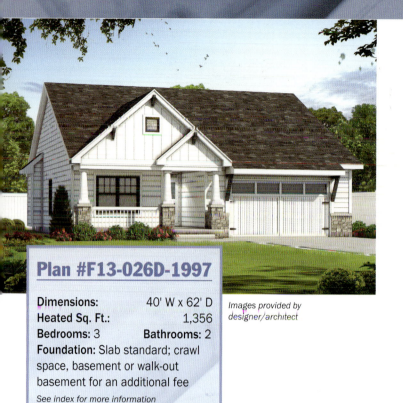

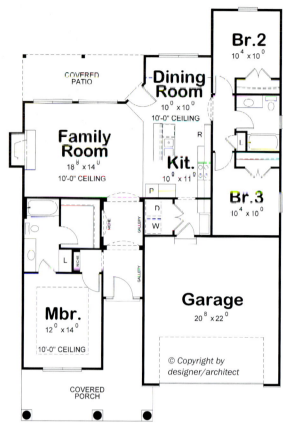

Plan #F13-026D-1997

Dimensions:	40' W x 62' D
Heated Sq. Ft.:	1,356
Bedrooms: 3	Bathrooms: 2

Foundation: Slab standard; crawl space, basement or walk-out basement for an additional fee

See index for more information

Images provided by designer/architect

Plan #F13-155D-0245

Dimensions:	74'6" W x 67'6" D
Heated Sq. Ft.:	2,383
Bedrooms: 3	Bathrooms: 3

Foundation: Crawl space or slab standard; basement or daylight basement for an additional fee

See index for more information

Images provided by designer/architect

Plan #F13-130D-0401

Dimensions: 33' W x 57'4" D
Heated Sq. Ft.: 1,563
Bedrooms: 3   **Bathrooms:** 2
Foundation: Slab standard; crawl space or basement for an additional fee

See index for more information

PORCH 16-4 x 8
9' Ceiling

LIVING ROOM 16 x 16
Vaulted Ceiling   Vaulted Ceiling

BED #1 16 x 12
9' Ceiling

Vaulted Ceiling   Vaulted Ceiling

DINING ROOM 16 x 11

Opt. Basement Stairs (deletes Pantry)

W D   A.C.   9' Ceiling

7' x 5' Island   DW Sink

HIS 5 x 5   Pantry   KITCHEN 16 x 11

HERS 7-8 x 4-6   Ref.

8' Ceiling

BED #2 12 x 11
9' Ceiling   FOYER   BED #3/ STUDY
Opt doors   12 x 10 plus
9' Ceiling

PORCH 22 x 6
9' Ceiling

© Copyright by designer/architect

Images provided by designer/architect

Plan #F13-011D-0658

Dimensions: 50' W x 52' D
Heated Sq. Ft.: 2,618
Bedrooms: 4   **Bathrooms:** 2½
Exterior Walls: 2" x 6"
Foundation: Crawl space or slab standard; basement for an additional fee

See index for more information

Second Floor 1,392 sq. ft.

BR. 4 11/0 X 12/2 (9' CLG.)

MECH   TILE SHWR   10/10 X 9/8 (9' CLG.)   SHLVS

VAULTED MASTER 14/0 X 18/10 +/-

14/8 X 6/6 +/-

LINEN

BR. 3 16/0 X 15/2 +/- (9' CLG.)   LINEN   DN.

BR. 2 11/0 X 14/10 (9' CLG.)   FOYER BELOW

First Floor 1,226 sq. ft.

REAR PORCH 30/0 X 12/0 +/-

SHOP 10/6 X 11/6   DINING 11/0 X 12/10 (9' CLG.)   GREAT RM. 18/0 X 18/10 (9' CLG.)

© Copyright by designer/architect

GARAGE 19/6 X 20/6

PANTRY 7/6 X 5/0 +/-   11/0 X 13/10 (9' CLG.)   UP

TWO STORY FOYER   DEN 10/0 X 11/2 (10' CLG.)

PORCH

Images provided by designer/architect

Plan #F13-155D-0247

Dimensions:	74'7" W x 70'6" D
Heated Sq. Ft.:	2,700
Bedrooms: 4	Bathrooms: 3

Foundation: Crawl space or slab standard; basement or daylight basement for an additional fee

See index for more information

Images provided by designer/architect

Plan #F13-084D-0086

Dimensions:	45'4" W x 76' D
Heated Sq. Ft.:	1,725
Bedrooms: 3	Bathrooms: 2

Foundation: Slab standard; crawl space for an additional fee

See index for more information

Images provided by designer/architect

Plan #F13-008D-0134

Dimensions: 28' W x 32' D
Heated Sq. Ft.: 1,275
Bedrooms: 4   **Bathrooms:** 2
Foundation: Basement standard; crawl space or slab for an additional fee

See index for more information

Images provided by designer/architect

Second Floor
443 sq. ft.

First Floor
832 sq. ft.

© Copyright by designer/architect

Plan #F13-121D-0025

Dimensions: 50' W x 34'6" D
Heated Sq. Ft.: 1,368
Bedrooms: 3   **Bathrooms:** 2
Foundation: Basement standard; crawl space or slab for an additional fee

See index for more information

Images provided by designer/architect

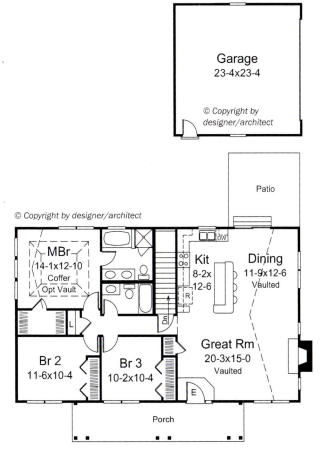

© Copyright by designer/architect

Plan #F13-051D-0960

Dimensions: 117' W x 50'8" D
Heated Sq. Ft.: 2,784
Bedrooms: 3   **Bathrooms:** 2
Exterior Walls: 2" x 6"
Foundation: Basement standard; crawl space or slab for an additional fee

See index for more information

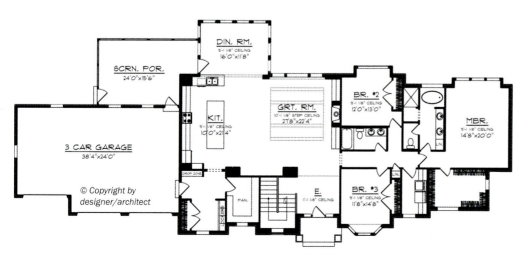

Features

- This Traditional ranch home design is sure to win you over with its very classy exterior
- You are welcomed into the home with eleven-foot ceilings that top the great room and kitchen
- All three bedrooms, including the master bedroom, are located to the right in the house
- The master bedroom includes a bath with a spa style tub, dual sinks, as well as a spacious walk-in closet
- The other two bedrooms share a centrally located bath
- The three-stall garage is located on the left side of the house with access to the large screened-in porch behind it
- 3-car front entry garage

Images provided by designer/architect

Plan #F13-084D-0094

Dimensions: 45'6" W x 85'4" D
Heated Sq. Ft.: 1,782
Bedrooms: 3 **Bathrooms:** 2
Foundation: Slab standard; crawl space for an additional fee

See index for more information

Features

- This one-story is terrific if you have a narrow lot and want a larger garage
- Enter from the covered front porch and find vaulted living area with fireplace
- The kitchen has an island that focuses on the living area when prepping a meal or cooking
- Off the garage is an organized mud room with walk-in pantry, built-in bench with cubbies, and a separate laundry room
- The dining area has lovely porch views
- The master bedroom has triple windows for a cheerful atmosphere and a huge spa style bath with a freestanding tub, oversized spa shower, two vanities, and a massive walk-in closet
- 2-car side entry garage plus a workshop

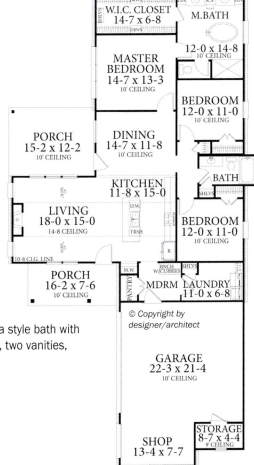

W.I.C. CLOSET 14-7 x 6-8
M.BATH 12-0 x 14-8 10' CEILING
MASTER BEDROOM 14-7 x 13-3 10' CEILING
BEDROOM 12-0 x 11-0 10' CEILING
PORCH 15-2 x 12-2 10' CEILING
DINING 14-7 x 11-8 10' CEILING
KITCHEN 11-8 x 15-0
BATH
LIVING 18-0 x 15-0 14-8 CEILING
BEDROOM 12-0 x 11-0 10' CEILING
10-8 CLG. LINE
PORCH 16-2 x 7-6 10' CEILING
PANTRY
MDRM
BNCH W/CUBBIES
LAUNDRY 11-0 x 6-8
© Copyright by designer/architect
GARAGE 22-3 x 21-4 10' CEILING
STORAGE 8-7 x 4-4 9' CEILING
SHOP 13-4 x 7-7

Images provided by designer/architect

Plan #F13-055D-1006

Dimensions: 101'8" W x 86'8" D
Heated Sq. Ft.: 3,752
Bonus Sq. Ft.: 677
Bedrooms: 4 **Bathrooms:** 3½
Foundation: Crawl space or slab standard; basement or daylight basement for an additional fee
See index for more information

Images provided by designer/architect

Features

- Stunning European manor home promises luxury living for every family member with spacious bedrooms and plenty of privacy
- The kitchen overlooks the expansive vaulted great room and has a massive island that seats up to six people comfortably
- The outdoor living area features a see-through fireplace it shares with the patio
- Near the garage is a kid's nook for staying organized, a safe room, a laundry room and friend's porch
- The bonus room has an additional 677 square feet of living area
- 3-car front entry garage

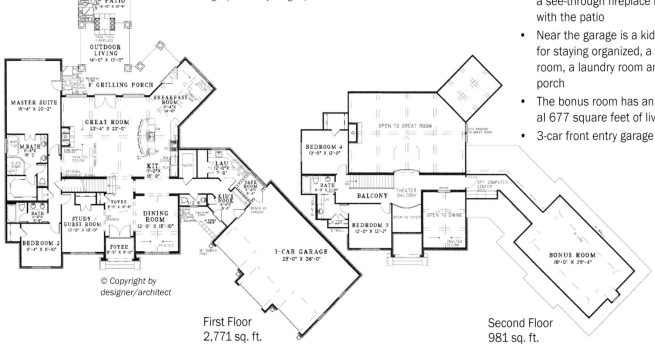

© Copyright by designer/architect

First Floor
2,771 sq. ft.

Second Floor
981 sq. ft.

Images provided by designer/architect

Plan #F13-101D-0050

Dimensions:	110'6" W x 84' D
Heated Sq. Ft.:	4,784
Bonus Sq. Ft.:	1,926
Bedrooms: 5	Bathrooms: 4½
Exterior Walls:	2" x 6"
Foundation:	Basement

Please see the index for more information

Features

- Rustic beams above the entry give this home a lodge feel
- The first floor enjoys an open floor plan that has the kitchen in the center of activity surrounded by the great room and casual dining area with a fireplace
- The private master bedroom and bath enjoy covered deck access and double walk-in closets
- A quiet home office is hidden behind the kitchen
- The second floor loft is a nice place to hang-out, and the laundry room is located near the second floor bedrooms for ease with this ongoing chore
- The optional lower level has an additional 1,926 square feet of living area and enjoys a wet bar and family room for entertaining, and for hobbies there's a climbing room and craft room
- 2-car side entry garage, and a 1-car front entry garage

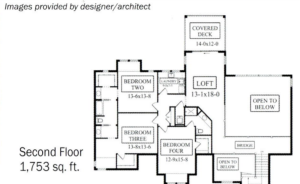

Second Floor
1,753 sq. ft.

© Copyright by designer/architect

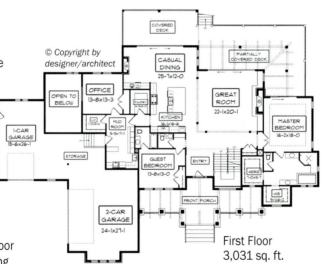

First Floor
3,031 sq. ft.

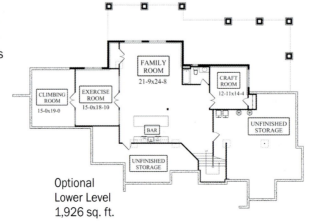

Optional
Lower Level
1,926 sq. ft.

houseplansandmore.com

Plan #F13-051D-0964

Dimensions: 103'8" W x 68'4" D
Heated Sq. Ft.: 4,206
Bedrooms: 5 **Bathrooms:** 4½
Exterior Walls: 2" x 6"
Foundation: Basement standard; crawl space or slab for an additional fee

See index for more information

Features

- This inviting Craftsman home offers some great extras for families including a mother-in-law suite on the first floor with its own bath and walk-in closet
- An open dining room extends off the kitchen and has direct access to the outdoor covered porch
- The master suite is positioned for privacy and features a pampering spa style bathroom and a large walk-in closet
- The cozy hearth room will be a lovely retreat, while the den near the front entry makes a great home office
- The kids will love the second floor play room
- 2-car front entry garage, and a 1-car side entry garage

Second Floor
1,259 sq. ft.

© Copyright by designer/architect

First Floor
2,947 sq. ft.

Images provided by designer/architect

© Copyright by designer/architect

Garage
21-4x19-8

Patio

Br 3
11-4x10-0

Great Rm
17-3x16-4
vaulted

Br 2
10-0x10-9

Bar

Hall

Kitchen
11-5x15-8

Laun.

Brk fst
13-6x11-0

Entry

Covered Porch

MBr
15-4x12-0
vaulted

Porch

Plan #F13-007D-0140

Dimensions: 62' W x 45' D
Heated Sq. Ft.: 1,591
Bedrooms: 3   **Bathrooms:** 2
Foundation: Basement standard;
crawl space or slab for an
additional fee

See index for more information

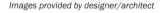

Images provided by designer/architect

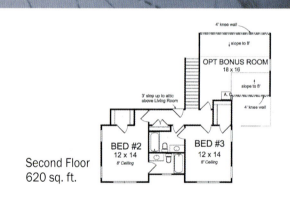

4' knee wall

slope to 8'

OPT BONUS ROOM
18 x 16

slope to 8'

3' step up to attic
above Living Room

4' knee wall

BED #2
12 x 14
8' Ceiling

BED #3
12 x 14
8' Ceiling

Second Floor
620 sq. ft.

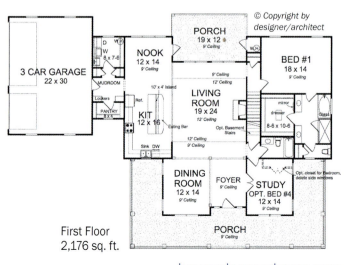

© Copyright by
designer/architect

3 CAR GARAGE
22 x 30

MUDROOM

NOOK
12 x 14
9' Ceiling

PORCH
19 x 12
9' Ceiling

BED #1
18 x 14
9' Ceiling

Lockers

PANTRY
8 x 4

KIT
12 x 16

10' x 4' Island

LIVING
ROOM
19 x 24
12' Ceiling

Opt. Basement
Stairs

mirror
dresser

8-6 x 10-6

DINING
ROOM
12 x 14
9' Ceiling

FOYER
9' Ceiling

STUDY
OPT. BED #4
12 x 14
9' Ceiling

First Floor
2,176 sq. ft.

PORCH
9' Ceiling

Plan #F13-130D-0335

Images provided by designer/architect

Dimensions: 84' W x 59' D
Heated Sq. Ft.: 2,796
Bonus Sq. Ft.: 316
Bedrooms: 4   **Bathrooms:** 4
Foundation: Slab standard; crawl
space or basement for an
additional fee

See index for more information

Plan #F13-077D-0043

Dimensions: 64' W x 45'10" D
Heated Sq. Ft.: 1,752
Bedrooms: 3   **Bathrooms:** 2
Foundation: Slab, crawl space, basement daylight basement or walk-out basement, please specify when ordering

See index for more information

Images provided by designer/architect

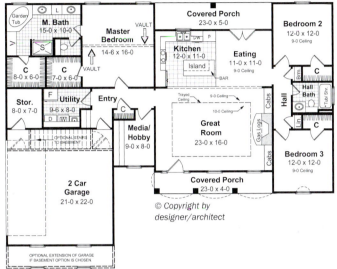

© Copyright by designer/architect

Plan #F13-011D-0754

Dimensions: 30' W x 70' D
Heated Sq. Ft.: 1,481
Bedrooms: 3   **Bathrooms:** 2
Exterior Walls: 2" x 6"
Foundation: Crawl space or slab standard; basement for an additional fee

See index for more information

Images provided by designer/architect

© Copyright by designer/architect

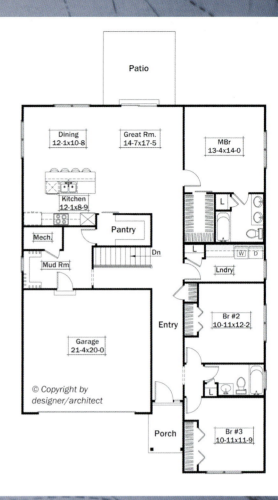

Plan #F13-169D-0002

Dimensions: 41' W x 60'4" D
Heated Sq. Ft.: 1,762
Bedrooms: 3   **Bathrooms:** 2
Foundation: Basement standard; crawl space or slab for an additional fee

See index for more information

Images provided by designer/architect

© Copyright by designer/architect

Plan #F13-172D-0031

Dimensions: 63' W x 43' D
Heated Sq. Ft.: 1,493
Bonus Sq. Ft.: 1,470
Bedrooms: 3   **Bathrooms:** 2
Exterior Walls: 2" x 6"
Foundation: Basement standard; crawl space, monolithic slab, stem wall slab, daylight basement or walk-out basement for an additional fee

See index for more information

Images provided by designer/architect

© Copyright by designer/architect

First Floor
1,493 sq. ft.

Optional
Lower Level
1,470 sq. ft.

Plan #F13-077D-0019

Dimensions: 54' W x 47' D
Heated Sq. Ft.: 1,400
Bedrooms: 3 **Bathrooms:** 2
Foundation: Slab, crawl space, basement or walk-out basement, please specify when ordering

See index for more information

Images provided by designer/architect

Plan #F13-028D-0076

Dimensions: 33' W x 36' D
Heated Sq. Ft.: 1,073
Bedrooms: 2 **Bathrooms:** 2
Foundation: Floating slab standard; monolithic slab, crawl space, basement or walk-out basement for an additional fee

See index for more information

Images provided by designer/architect

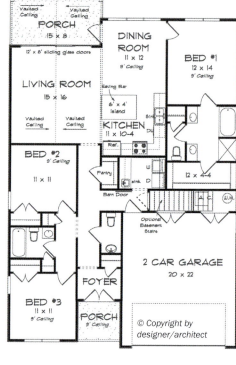

Plan #F13-130D-0406

Dimensions: 39' W x 58' D
Heated Sq. Ft.: 1,483
Bedrooms: 3   **Bathrooms:** 2½
Foundation: Slab standard; crawl space or basement for an additional fee

See index for more information

Images provided by designer/architect

First Floor
2,067 sq. ft.

Optional
Second Floor
379 sq. ft.

Plan #F13-077D-0142

Dimensions: 70' W x 56' D
Heated Sq. Ft.: 2,067
Bonus Sq. Ft.: 379
Bedrooms: 3   **Bathrooms:** 2½
Foundation: Slab or crawl space, please specify when ordering; for basement version see Plan #077D-0164 at houseplansandmore.com

Please see the index for more information

Images provided by designer/architect

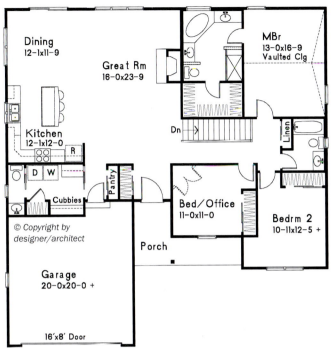

Plan #F13-058D-0255

Dimensions: 52' W x 53' D
Heated Sq. Ft.: 1,819
Bedrooms: 3   Bathrooms: 2½
Foundation: Basement

See index for more information

Images provided by designer/architect

Dining
12-1x11-9

Great Rm
16-0x23-9

MBr
13-0x16-9
Vaulted Clg

Kitchen
12-1x12-0

Dn

Linen

Pantry

Cubbies

Bed/Office
11-0x11-0

Bedrm 2
10-11x12-5 +

© Copyright by designer/architect

Porch

Garage
20-0x20-0 +

16'x8' Door

Plan #F13-076D-0235

Dimensions: 50' W x 55' D
Heated Sq. Ft.: 2,291
Bedrooms: 4   Bathrooms: 3
Foundation: Basement, crawl space or slab, please specify when ordering

See index for more information

Images provided by designer/architect

Second Floor
527 sq. ft.

BEDROOM 4
13-6 X 12-6

DOWN

CLOS

BEDROOM 3
12-6 X 12-6

ATTIC STORAGE

ATTIC STORAGE

MASTER SUITE
16 X 13

BREAKFAST
12 X 11-6

OPTIONAL COVERED TERRACE
13 X 13

HER CLOS

MASTER BATH

PAN

COOK

FAMILY ROOM
17-6 X 19

VAULT

VAULT

HIS CLOSET

UTILITY

DROP ZONE

REF

BAR TOP

© Copyright by designer/architect

GARAGE
20 X 21

DINING ROOM
12 X 12

COAT

BATH

CLOSET

FOYER

BEDROOM 2
12-3 X 12

PORCH

First Floor
1,764 sq. ft.

Plan #F13-001D-0067

Dimensions: 48' W x 37'8" D
Heated Sq. Ft.: 1,285
Bedrooms: 3 **Bathrooms:** 2
Foundation: Crawl space standard; basement or slab for an additional fee

See index for more information

Images provided by designer/architect

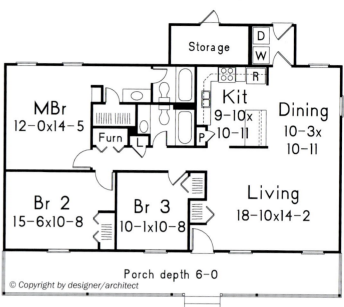

Storage

D
W

MBr
12-0x14-5

Furn

Kit
9-10x
10-11

R
P
L

Dining
10-3x
10-11

Br 2
15-6x10-8

Br 3
10-1x10-8

Living
18-10x14-2

Porch depth 6-0

Plan #F13-088D-0540

Dimensions: 55' W x 38'11" D
Heated Sq. Ft.: 2,281
Bonus Sq. Ft.: 1,086
Bedrooms: 3 **Bathrooms:** 2½
Exterior Walls: 2" x 6"
Foundation: Daylight basement

See index for more information

Images provided by designer/architect

Second Floor
845 sq. ft.

STORAGE · LOFT AREA 20' X 17'9" · BATH · STORAGE
BDRM. #2 12'X18'1" · BDRM.#3 12'X18'1"
DOWN
STORAGE · OPEN TO BELOW · STORAGE

First Floor
1,436 sq. ft.

COVERED ENTRY PORCH
FOYER 6'X14' · UTILITY RM. · PANTRY
M. BATH · WIC · WIC
KITCHEN 13' X 13'6"
WIC · SUN RM. 7'6" X18'
DOWN · UP
MASTER SUITE 12' X 15'10" · GREAT ROOM 20' X 17' · DINING ROOM 12' X12'5"
DECK AREA · DECK AREA

Optional Lower Level
1,086 sq. ft.

RETAINING WALL
UP
2-CAR GARAGE 20' X 26'10"
UNFINISHED BASEMENT
CONCRETE PATIO

Detached Garage
23-4x23-4

© Copyright by
designer/architect

Patio

MBr
13-4x16-4
Vaulted

Kit/ Dining
19-8x11-0
Vaulted

Great Rm
17-8x14-0
Vaulted

Br 2
11-8x10-0

Br 3
10-11x10-8

Covered Porch

Plan #F13-121D-0031

Dimensions: 46' W x 36' D
Heated Sq. Ft.: 1,308
Bedrooms: 3   Bathrooms: 2
Foundation: Basement standard;
crawl space or slab for an
additional fee

See index for more information

Images provided by designer/architect

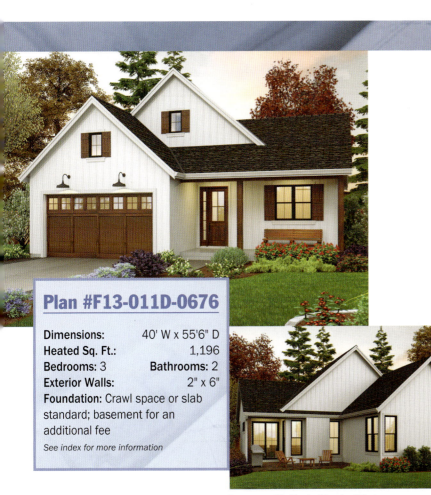

Plan #F13-011D-0676

Dimensions: 40' W x 55'6" D
Heated Sq. Ft.: 1,196
Bedrooms: 3   Bathrooms: 2
Exterior Walls: 2" x 6"
Foundation: Crawl space or slab
standard; basement for an
additional fee

See index for more information

Images provided by designer/architect

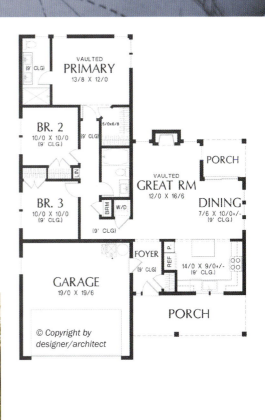

VAULTED
PRIMARY
13/8 X 12/0
(9' CLG)

BR. 2
10/0 X 10/0
(9' CLG.)

BR. 3
10/0 X 10/0
(9' CLG.)

VAULTED
GREAT RM
12/0 X 16/6

PORCH

DINING
7/6 X 10/0+/-
(9' CLG.)

FOYER
(9' CLG)

14/0 X 9/0+/-
(9' CLG.)

GARAGE
19/0 X 19/6

PORCH

© Copyright by
designer/architect

Plan #F13-155D-0134

Dimensions: 70'6" W x 56'2" D
Heated Sq. Ft.: 2,031
Bonus Sq. Ft.: 406
Bedrooms: 3 **Bathrooms:** 2½
Foundation: Crawl space or slab standard; basement or daylight basement for an additional fee

See index for more information

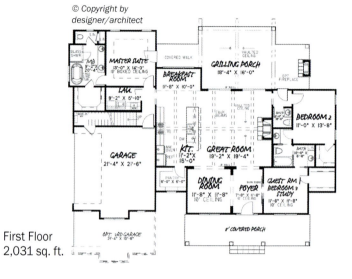

Optional
Second Floor
406 sq. ft.

First Floor
2,031 sq. ft.

Plan #F13-167D-0010

Dimensions: 70'11" W x 84'10" D
Heated Sq. Ft.: 3,409
Bedrooms: 4 **Bathrooms:** 4½
Exterior Walls: 2" x 6"
Foundation: Crawl space standard; slab for an additional fee

See index for more information

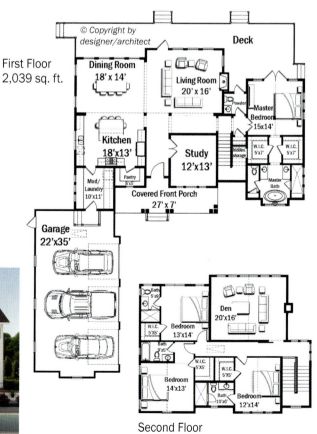

First Floor
2,039 sq. ft.

Second Floor
1,370 sq. ft.

Images provided by designer/architect

© Copyright by
designer/architect

Plan #F13-058D-0240

Dimensions:	55' W x 46' D
Heated Sq. Ft.:	1,594
Bedrooms: 3	Bathrooms: 2
Foundation:	Basement

See index for more information

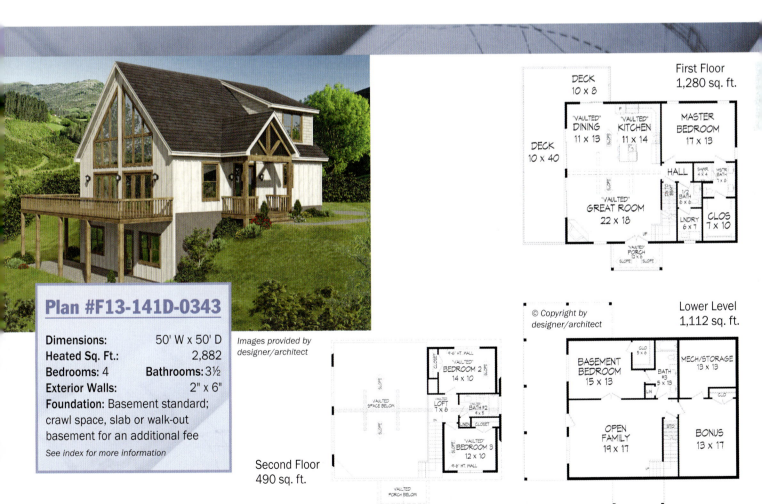

Images provided by designer/architect

© Copyright by
designer/architect

Plan #F13-141D-0343

Dimensions:	50' W x 50' D
Heated Sq. Ft.:	2,882
Bedrooms: 4	Bathrooms: 3½
Exterior Walls:	2" x 6"

Foundation: Basement standard;
crawl space, slab or walk-out
basement for an additional fee

See index for more information

Plan #F13-167D-0011

Dimensions:	84'11" W x 74'6" D
Heated Sq. Ft.:	3,413
Bedrooms:	4
Bathrooms:	3 full, 2 half
Foundation:	Slab standard; crawl space for an additional fee

See index for more information

Features

- This open floor plan design offers great modern style living with a utility/craft space, perfect for the homeowners who love fun hands-on projects
- The kitchen enjoys a large island with casual dining space for up to five people to dine comfortably
- The primary suite enjoys its own en-suite bath with two vanities, a separate toilet room, a huge spa style shower, and a walk-in dressing room style closet
- The office is designed for peace and quiet with double doors off the foyer
- A gameroom/media room has a built-in wet bar and direct access onto the covered vaulted patio with an outdoor kitchen
- 3-car side entry garage

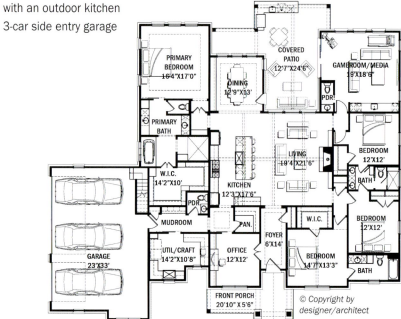

© Copyright by designer/architect

Images provided by designer/architect

houseplansandmore.com

Plan #F13-032D-1178

Dimensions:	48' W x 40' D
Heated Sq. Ft.:	2,294
Bonus Sq. Ft.:	336
Bedrooms: 3	**Bathrooms:** 2½
Exterior Walls:	2" x 6"

Foundation: Basement standard; crawl space, floating slab or monolithic slab for an additional fee

See index for more information

Features

- Rustic Craftsman details and Modern Farmhouse architecture collide to form a home that feels fresh, inviting and easy to come home to
- Enter the foyer and find a large mud room on the left with tons of ways to stay organized
- The kitchen has a large island and to the left an open dining area
- The second floor has an ultra private master suite with large bath featuring a freestanding tub, and a huge spa shower
- The optional bonus room has an additional 336 square feet of living area
- 1-car front entry garage

STORAGE
12'-0" X 26'-8"

Second Floor
554 sq. ft.

WALK-IN 6'-4" X 4'-8"

WALK-IN 6'-4" X 5'-6"

MASTER BEDROOM 11'-8" X 12'-8"

BATH ROOM 17'-4" X 7'-8"

SHELVES

Lower Level
870 sq. ft.

FAMILY ROOM 17'-0" X 11'-8"

BEDROOM #3 12'-4" X 10'-0"

BEDROOM #2 12'-4" X 10'-8"

LAUNDRY ROOM 6'-6" X 6'-2"

First Floor
870 sq. ft.

CATHEDRAL CEILING

LIVING ROOM 17'-8" X 12'-0"

TERRACE 12'-0" X 12'-0"

DINING ROOM 12'-2" X 12'-8"

GARAGE 16'-8" X 26'-8"

KITCHEN 13'-10" X 12'-8"

MUDROOM 10'-0" X 8'-6"

FOYER 10'-4" X 8'-8"

PANTRY 4'-10" X 5'-4"

BENCH

STOOP 30'-0" X 4'-0"

© Copyright by designer/architect

Images provided by designer/architect

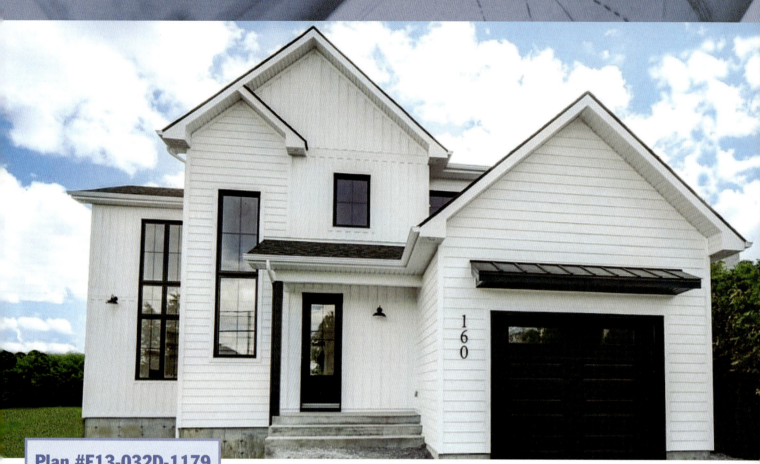

Plan #F13-032D-1179

Dimensions:	46' W x 40' D
Heated Sq. Ft.:	1,583
Bonus Sq. Ft.:	872
Bedrooms: 3	**Bathrooms:** 1½
Exterior Walls:	2" x 6"

Foundation: Basement standard; crawl space, floating slab or monolithic slab for an additional fee

See index for more information

Second Floor
711 sq. ft.

© Copyright by designer/architect

Optional
Lower Level
872 sq. ft.

First Floor
872 sq. ft.

Features

- Modern style home has one-of-a-kind curb appeal thanks to the use of vertical two-story windows on the exterior
- The first floor features an open layout most coveted by homeowners today including a kitchen with a walk-in pantry and large island with dining space
- The second floor houses all of the bedrooms to ensure privacy from the main gathering spaces
- The optional lower level has an additional 872 square feet of living area
- 1-car front entry garage

Plan #F13-101D-0125

Dimensions:	118'3" W x 70' D
Heated Sq. Ft.:	2,970
Bonus Sq. Ft.:	2,014
Bedrooms: 2	Bathrooms: 2½
Exterior Walls:	2" x 6"
Foundation:	Walk-out basement

See index for more information

Features

- This rustic modern masterpiece offers an open concept floor plan with the utmost style and distinction
- Step into the foyer and be greeted by an open and expansive great room topped with a stunning ceiling
- The bright and stylish kitchen has a huge island, rustic beams above and plenty of cabinetspace for maintaining a sleek appearance free of clutter
- The first floor master bedroom enjoys a beamed ceiling, covered deck access, a luxury bath and a huge walk-in closet
- A guest room with its own private bath can be found on the opposite side of the first floor from the master bedroom for extra privacy
- The optional lower level has an additional 2,014 square feet of living area including a wet bar with island, a rec room, a game nook, three additional bedrooms, one full bath and a half bath
- 2-car front entry garage, and a 1-car side entry garage

Images provided by designer/architect

Optional Lower Level
2,014 sq. ft.

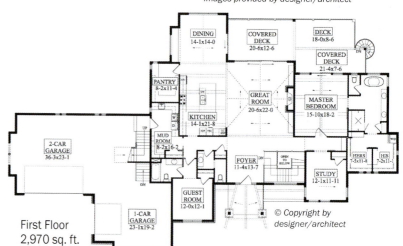

First Floor
2,970 sq. ft.

© Copyright by designer/architect

Creating Curb Appeal
making your home stand-out from the crowd

Everyone wants to own that home on a street that stops people in their tracks. No, that doesn't mean it has to be a huge mansion with jaw-dropping over-the-top features, it means it just has that "thing" called curb appeal that makes it feel warm and inviting, and seems to beg neighbors and friends to come on in. Below are some of the most popular ways to create that home "eye-candy" we all dream of.

exciting entries

Gone are the days of cookie-cutter front porch entries. Today's homeowners love showing off their personality and making front porches a precursor to what guests will find inside. These entrances often include statement lighting, custom doors, unique surrounding windows, luxurious plant holders and even seating. Homeowners are really trying to pull you in and they are making these spaces comfortable for outdoor relaxation, too. Front doors made of glass or that are oversized are becoming more popular. Fun, playful colors are also being introduced. If you're building a European style home, then ornate iron and glass style doors are a beautiful option. For those building a Craftsman home, many front doors include glass windows in a variety of shapes and sizes traditional to the Arts & Crafts style movement. Another playful option is the Dutch door. A Dutch door allows half of the door to be open at anytime, whether it's the top, or the bottom. It's a great way to get some fresh air moving through your home on a nice day.

little extras = big impact

Just like it's being seen in the interior with statement lighting, there is a current statement being made on the exterior, too. Statement house numbers are all the rage and people are getting super creative in how they're displaying their home's address numbers. Adhered or added to modern planters, custom painted in a unique font on the front door, or positioned in a clever place on the front facade, house numbers are actually adding style to a home's exterior whatever its architectural style. No longer a necessity or eyesore, these numbers are enhancing the front of a home and are carefully taking homage to the home's architectural style. A thoughtfully selected style and finish can greatly enhance the authenticity of your home's architecture. Have fun, and be playful with it. It definitely allows you show off you and your home's personality and style.

bright is alright

Bright colors on home exteriors if they fit with the architectural style are still being seen. But, some styles like Craftsman, are still utilizing more neutral tones. Darker paint colors are also making a comeback on the exterior, and in complete contrast, off-white and white exteriors are also growing in popularity just like white has made a major comeback in interior home décor.

custom doors, need we say more?

What used to be a pretty basic element to a home's front facade, the front door was often just a plain solid door meant for security purposes only. The doors homeowners are selecting today are thoughtful, well planned exterior ornamentation. Once again, they carry through with the home's architecture and often include many windows in unusual shapes, which add plenty of extra light to the interior. Take it one step further and paint the door (inside and out) in a vibrant color and add unique house numbers for the perfect expression that's friendly and inviting.

the vintage advantage

Vintage flair hasn't waned, either especially since the pandemic made finding new furniture impossible. Luckily, antique and thrift shops provide plenty of great options that are "new to you." Offering a casual and inviting element to a covered front porch, fun vintage pieces like re-purposed benches, antique watering cans, or unusual planters offer a kitschy element that's fun, playful, and asks guests to sit down, strike up a conversation, and stay awhile.

nostalgic for front porches

Years ago, the front porch was the gathering place where people would mingle and socialize with neighbors. It was one of the only ways to stay connected with those around them and it provided a space for enjoying the outdoors. This trend is reappearing as lot sizes are becoming smaller and homeowners are interested more than ever in outdoor living spaces. Often, the covered front porch is one of the only outdoor spaces and because of this, people are using this space to the fullest by adding furniture, lighting, and other elements that make it feel comfortable and warm.

sidewalk talk

With all of the thought that goes into every little detail of your home's design, you would think by the time the landscaping and hardscapes have to be determined you can finally relax and not worry so much about the aesthetics of these elements. But, that truly isn't so! Sidewalk design is being carried through with a home's architectural style and color palette as it offers the initial welcome to guests. Don't get lazy when it comes to your sidewalk. You will see that a carefully designed walkway will pave the way for a major curb appeal moment. Today's homeowners are opting for pavers, stone, or other materials for their home's main entrance. And, due to the efficiency and affordability of LED light bulbs lining those paths and walkways with light add curb appeal at night for a very low cost.

sensing a pattern

Driveways, much like sidewalks can offer little or no added style to a home if you choose not to take them into account. But, homeowners today love the look of patterned driveways that either match the sidewalk or complement it. Have fun using textures and materials that complement your home's exterior and it will positively impact curb appeal.

flora forever

Flowers and plants are more popular than ever for surrounding your home's facade and adding softness. Landscape designers of today are thoughtful in their plant choices. Native landscaping is the way to go. Selecting plants that naturally grow in your region allows for less watering and fertilization, which is better for the environment. Choosing native plants also goes in line with the trend that homeowners are pairing down their ecological footprint. Native plants require less water than what is already received in rainfall. Plus, less sprinkler time means lower water bills, less water waste, and all around happier plants.

lighter landscaping

Being paired down to reflect the less cluttered style of homes being designed today, landscaping especially in the front of a home is much less fussy than in previous years. Today, homeowners are choosing not to over plant shrubs and trees. Think clean, well-manicured lawns, carefully selected bushes, and tree options that are well suited with the home's architecture. By reducing the amount of landscaping a yard has, homeowners are staying eco-friendly creating less erosion issues, too.

So, by using less, your choices are now more important in order to make an impact. Choose plants that complement the color scheme of your home. If your home is gray, then offset it with pinks and reds. Or, if you've chosen a dark blue or slate, then white and yellow can provide that pop of color, or brighten the exterior. Another fun option is to select edible landscape such as colorful pepper plants and herbs and suddenly your landscaping is working twice as hard as your own organic garden, too. This is especially a great idea if you lack backyard space, or the position of the front of your home has more sunlight, making it more suitable to successful gardening.

more than just a pretty pot

The planters on the market today have really come a long way. These vessels that used to just hold flowers can now often upstage their contents. Uniquely shaped, and often in a style that complements a home's architecture, a well chosen and placed planter can add immense curb appeal.

see the light

Transom windows are being added to the front exterior and around the entire perimeter of a home for several reasons. First, they add character to the facade in a clean, uncomplicated way, that is in line with Craftsman and Mid-Century modern style that is quite popular right now. They have a less formal feel, than an arched window design. And, they are adding additional light to the interior, which is a feature currently popular in interior home design. Open airy interiors are dictating home design, so the addition of larger windows makes an interior feel more open especially in homes with smaller square footages. Also, large picture windows are being seen in every style of home from Craftsman to Mid-Century Modern, and everything in between.

Exterior lighting adds drama once the sky goes dark. Even a solar light placed strategically on a unique ornamental tree can enhance your exterior and draw eyes to want to see more. Or, take it a step further and create a facade lit with soffit lighting, or light the bottom corners of the home for intensified drama. Many of these lighting systems can now be controlled right from your smart phone making it easy to use and creating added security when you're away.

Unless noted, copyright by designer/architect; Page 86, top, left to right: Light up the night, Plan #013S-0014; Easy to maintain native plants stay greener, Plan #106S-0070; Great use of native plants, Plan #011S-0206; middle: Less is more landscaping, Plan #101D-0061, Warren Diggles Photography; bottom, left to right: Planters that make an impact, Plan #101D-0059, Warren Diggles Photography; These planters steal the show, Plan #072S-0002; Page 87, bottom, left: Exterior lighting done right, Plan #32D-1067; top, left to right: Great door details, Plan #111D-0018; Unique large transom, Plan #011S-0003; bottom, right: Carefully determined decor, Plan #101D-0052, Damon Searles, photographer. See additional photos and purchase plans at houseplansandmore.com.

the finish line

Depending on how luxurious the home is, those with larger budgets are using copper gutters to add curb appeal and style that truly stands out. Another interesting addition can be a unique fence that features an artistic pattern that basically becomes a work of art. Choosing a fence style with a similar architectural feel will make your home seem thoughtfully planned.

As homeowners tastes change, so do their ideas of what the ideal architectural style truly is. As their need for less complicated living, free of clutter and visual distractions becomes more important, the popular architectural styles reflect that. If they're craving a need to feel one with nature, then their desired style of home will turn to architecture that allows nature to be honored and respected. These constant shifts in tastes and trends in society are what make the landscape around us so colorful and interesting with glimpses of the past, present and future found all around us in any given city or neighborhood. Whatever style of architecture you choose, remember these curb appeal tips for optimizing the exterior style to the fullest and making your personality and home shine wherever it is that you live.

Plan #F13-084D-0095

Dimensions: 64'4" W x 74'1" D
Heated Sq. Ft.: 2,298
Bedrooms: 4 **Bathrooms:** 2½
Foundation: Slab standard; crawl space for an additional fee
See index for more information

Images provided by designer/architect

Features

- Stylish Country French elegance in a one-story floor; this home offers a beautiful exterior with so much curb appeal, you'll be begging to see the inside when you reach the front door
- Step into the foyer and see the dining area to the right topped with a 12' ceiling
- The living area straight ahead has a beamed 12' ceiling, double doors to a covered porch and a cozy fireplace
- The kitchen enjoys an open layout with an island, a walk-in pantry, and even a built-in desk
- A split bedroom layout has the entrance of the master bedroom separated from the other bedrooms for privacy
- 2-car side entry garage

Porch no. 2

KITCHEN
DINING
12-0 x 16-6

BEDROOM 1
13-0 x 14-4

BEDROOM 2
13-0 x 12-0

GREAT ROOM
20-0 x 14-0

Porch no. 1

© Copyright by
designer/architect

Plan #F13-028D-0084

Dimensions: 33' W x 42' D
Heated Sq. Ft.: 1,122
Bedrooms: 2   **Bathrooms:** 2
Foundation: Floating slab standard; monolithic slab, crawl space, basement or walk-out basement for an additional fee

See index for more information

Images provided by designer/architect

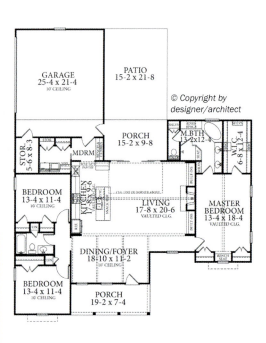

GARAGE
25-4 x 21-4
10' CEILING

PATIO
15-2 x 21-8

© Copyright by
designer/architect

STOR.
5-6 x 8-3

PORCH
15-2 x 9-8

M.BTH
13-2 x 12-4

W.I.C.
6-8 x 12-4

BEDROOM
13-4 x 11-4
10' CEILING

KITCHEN
14-8 x 9-6

LIVING
17-8 x 20-6
VAULTED CLG.

MASTER
BEDROOM
13-4 x 18-4
VAULTED CLG.

DINING/FOYER
18-10 x 11-2
10' CEILING

BEDROOM
13-4 x 11-4
10' CEILING

PORCH
19-2 x 7-4

Plan #F13-084D-0091

Dimensions: 59' W x 68'2" D
Heated Sq. Ft.: 1,936
Bedrooms: 3   **Bathrooms:** 2
Foundation: Slab standard; crawl space for an additional fee

See index for more information

Images provided by designer/architect

Plan #F13-111D-0117

Dimensions: 68' W x 82' D
Heated Sq. Ft.: 3,228
Bedrooms: 4   **Bathrooms:** 2½
Foundation: Slab standard; crawl space for an additional fee

See index for more information

Second Floor 1,507 sq. ft.

First Floor 1,721 sq. ft.

© Copyright by designer/architect

Images provided by designer/architect

Plan #F13-088D-0544

Dimensions: 46' W x 35'10" D
Heated Sq. Ft.: 1,781
Bonus Sq. Ft.: 1,436
Bedrooms: 3   **Bathrooms:** 2½
Exterior Walls: 2" x 6"
Foundation: Daylight basement

See index for more information

Second Floor 345 sq. ft.

© Copyright by designer/architect

Images provided by designer/architect

Optional Lower Level 1,436 sq. ft.

First Floor 1,436 sq. ft.

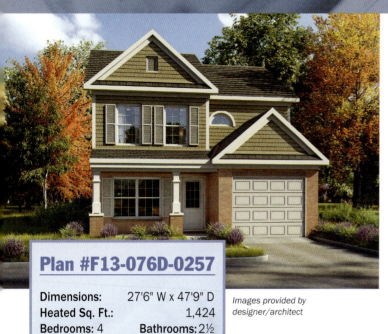

Second Floor
550 sq. ft.

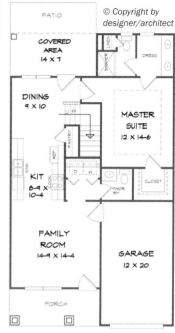

© Copyright by
designer/architect

First Floor
874 sq. ft.

Plan #F13-076D-0257

Dimensions:	27'6" W x 47'9" D
Heated Sq. Ft.:	1,424
Bedrooms: 4	Bathrooms: 2½
Foundation:	Slab

See index for more information

*Images provided by
designer/architect*

Plan #F13-007D-0029

Dimensions:	24' W x 30' D
Heated Sq. Ft.:	576
Bedrooms: 1	Bathrooms: 1
Foundation: Crawl space standard;
slab for an additional fee	

See index for more information

*Images provided by
designer/architect*

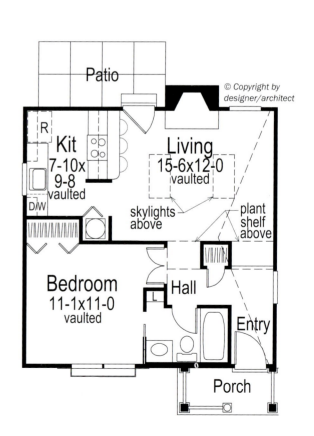

© Copyright by
designer/architect

Plan #F13-052D-0157

Dimensions:	40'4" W x 42' D
Heated Sq. Ft.:	2,067
Bonus Sq. Ft.:	356
Bedrooms: 4	Bathrooms: 2½
Foundation:	Basement

See index for more information

Images provided by designer/architect

Second Floor
860 sq. ft.

© Copyright by designer/architect

Bath 2

Bedrm. 2
13² x 12⁶

Bedrm. 3
11¹⁰ x 13⁶

Bedrm. 4
13² x 13⁶

Open to Living Area

Down

Deck
16⁶ x 12⁰

Pant.

Kitchen
18⁰ x 11⁴

Master Bath
Tub · Shower · Lav.

WIC

Dining

Master Bedroom
15⁶ x 15⁶

Living Area
18⁰ x 21⁸

Front Porch
38⁰ x 8⁰

First Floor
1,119 sq. ft.

Three Car Garage
20¹⁰ x 33⁰

Flex Room
15² x 23⁰

Up

Furn. · Wh. · Cls.

Lower Level
88 sq. ft.

Plan #F13-126D-1175

Dimensions:	28' W x 26' D
Heated Sq. Ft.:	910
Bedrooms: 2	Bathrooms: 1½
Exterior Walls:	2" x 6"
Foundation:	Slab

See index for more information

Images provided by designer/architect

9'-2"x11'-0"
2,79x3,35

13'-0"x13'-8"
3,96x4,17

11'-0"x12'-8"
3,35x3,86

Second Floor
494 sq. ft.

11'-0''x12'-6''
3,35x3,81

11'-6''x24'-6''
3,51x7,47

11'-0''x12'-0''
3,35x3,66

First Floor
416 sq. ft.

© Copyright by designer/architect

Plan #F13-011D-0674

Dimensions: 40' W x 60'6" D
Heated Sq. Ft.: 1,552
Bedrooms: 3   **Bathrooms:** 2
Exterior Walls: 2" x 6"
Foundation: Crawl space or slab standard; basement for an additional fee

See index for more information

Images provided by designer/architect

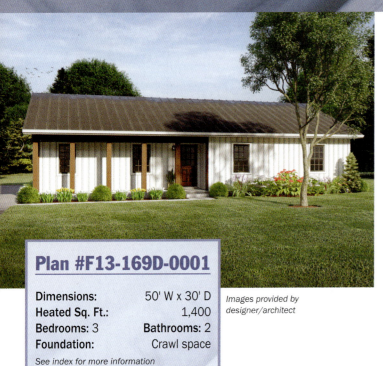

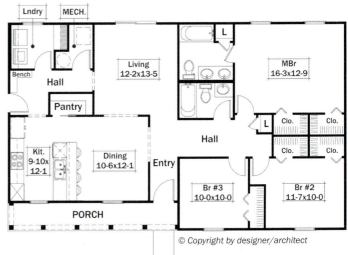

Plan #F13-169D-0001

Dimensions: 50' W x 30' D
Heated Sq. Ft.: 1,400
Bedrooms: 3   **Bathrooms:** 2
Foundation: Crawl space

See index for more information

Images provided by designer/architect

Images provided by
designer/architect

Plan #F13-144D-0024

Dimensions: 32' W x 32' D
Heated Sq. Ft.: 1,024
Bedrooms: 1   **Bathrooms:** 1½
Exterior Walls: 2" x 6"
Foundation: Crawl space, slab, or basement standard; walk-out basement for an additional fee

See index for more information

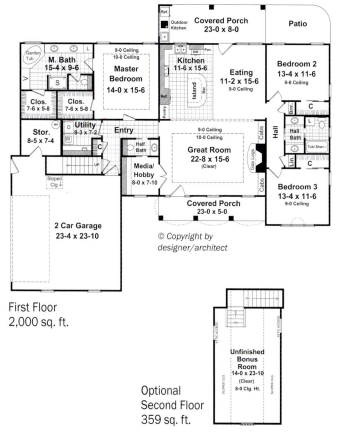

Images provided by
designer/architect

First Floor
2,000 sq. ft.

Optional Second Floor
359 sq. ft.

Plan #F13-077D-0128

Dimensions: 69' W x 59'10" D
Heated Sq. Ft.: 2,000
Bonus Sq. Ft.: 359
Bedrooms: 3   **Bathrooms:** 2½
Foundation: Crawl space or slab, please specify when ordering; for basement version, see Plan #077D-0131 at houseplansandmore.com

See index for more information

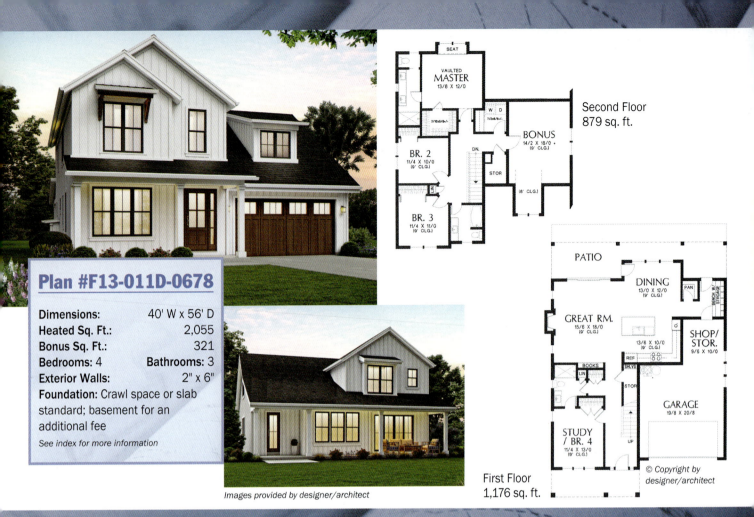

Plan #F13-011D-0678

Dimensions:	40' W x 56' D
Heated Sq. Ft.:	2,055
Bonus Sq. Ft.:	321
Bedrooms: 4	**Bathrooms:** 3
Exterior Walls:	2" x 6"

Foundation: Crawl space or slab standard; basement for an additional fee

See index for more information

Second Floor
879 sq. ft.

First Floor
1,176 sq. ft.

© Copyright by designer/architect

Images provided by designer/architect

Plan #F13-101D-0162

Dimensions:	58' W x 73' D
Heated Sq. Ft.:	2,017
Bedrooms: 2	**Bathrooms:** 2
Exterior Walls:	2" x 6"
Foundation:	Crawl space

See index for more information

© Copyright by designer/architect

Images provided by designer/architect

houseplansandmore.com

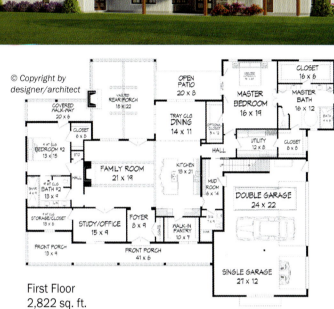

Plan #F13-141D-0533

Dimensions:	89'9" W x 66'5" D
Heated Sq. Ft.:	3,665
Bedrooms: 2	Bathrooms: 4
Exterior Walls:	2" x 6"

Foundation: Crawl space or slab, please specify when ordering

See index for more information

Images provided by designer/architect

© Copyright by designer/architect

Second Floor
843 sq. ft.

First Floor
2,822 sq. ft.

© Copyright by designer/architect

Plan #F13-051D-0982

Dimensions:	79'11" W x 69'6" D
Heated Sq. Ft.:	2,150
Bedrooms: 3	Bathrooms: 2½
Exterior Walls:	2" x 6"

Foundation: Basement standard; crawl space or slab for an additional fee

See index for more information

Images provided by designer/architect

Plan #F13-155D-0148

Dimensions:	72'6" W x 64'8" D
Heated Sq. Ft.:	1,897
Bonus Sq. Ft.:	395
Bedrooms: 4	Bathrooms: 2

Foundation: Crawl space or slab standard; basement or daylight basement for an additional fee

See index for more information

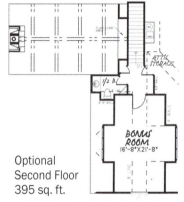

Optional Second Floor 395 sq. ft.

First Floor 1,897 sq. ft.

Plan #F13-007D-0134

Dimensions:	73'8" W x 32' D
Heated Sq. Ft.:	1,310
Bedrooms: 3	Bathrooms: 2

Foundation: Basement standard; crawl space or slab for an additional fee

See index for more information

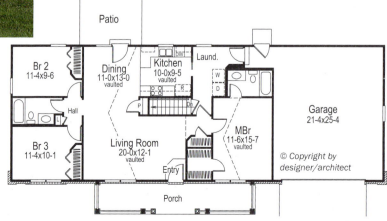

Second Floor
843 sq. ft.

Br.2
11⁰ x 12⁴

Loft
10⁹ x 12⁴

DN

Br.3
11⁰ x 12⁸

Br.4
12⁰ x 11⁰

COVERED PATIO

Suite
14⁸ x 14⁰
11'-0" CEILING

Eating Area
11⁰ x 11⁰

Family Room
14⁰ x 19⁸
11'-0" CEILING

Kit.
11⁰ x 12⁶

STORAGE UNDER STAIRS

DROP ZONE

UP

© Copyright by designer/architect

Garage
21⁰ x 22⁸/34⁰

Flex Room
12⁰ x 11⁰

COVERED PORCH

First Floor
1,594 sq. ft.

Plan #F13-026D-2161

Dimensions: 41' W x 68' D
Heated Sq. Ft.: 2,437
Bedrooms: 4   **Bathrooms:** 4
Foundation: Slab standard; crawl space, basement or walk-out basement for an additional fee

See index for more information

Images provided by designer/architect

ATTIC

MECH. CLST.

BEDROOM 4
12⁰ x 10⁸

MEDIA
13² x 15⁸

Second Floor
1,332 sq. ft.

BEDROOM 3
13⁰ x 11⁰

BATH 2

WET BAR

BATH 3

BEDROOM 2
13⁰ x 11⁰

GAMEROOM
17⁰ x 18⁸

© Copyright by designer/architect

M BATH

COVERED PATIO

MASTER BEDROOM
13⁸ x 17⁴

LIVING
17⁴ x 17⁰

WIC

STOR

UTILITY
8⁴ x 6¹⁰

MUD

PWDR

NICHE

DINING
17⁴ x 8⁸

STUDY
18⁰ x 23⁶

KITCHEN
13⁰ x 10⁴

ENTRY

STUDY
13⁰ x 11⁰

PORCH

First Floor
1,663 sq. ft.

Plan #F13-111D-0111

Dimensions: 41'1" W x 68'6" D
Heated Sq. Ft.: 2,995
Bedrooms: 4   **Bathrooms:** 3½
Foundation: Slab standard; crawl space or basement for an additional fee

See index for more information

Images provided by designer/architect

Plan #F13-101D-0057

Dimensions:	58' W x 90' D
Heated Sq. Ft.:	2,037
Bonus Sq. Ft.:	1,330
Bedrooms: 1	Bathrooms: 1½
Exterior Walls:	2" x 6"
Foundation:	Walk-out basement

See index for more information

Features

- Enjoy the outdoors on both floors with first floor covered and open decks and a lower level patio
- The front porch opens to an entry hall with a formal dining room and a staircase to the lower level nearby
- The large U-shaped kitchen features space for casual dining as well as a wet bar for entertaining
- The master bedroom is in a wing to itself and features a stepped ceiling, a luxurious bath, and a large walk-in closet
- The optional lower level has an additional 1,330 square feet of living area and offers two additional bedrooms with baths, an office, an open recreation space, a safe room, and unfinished storage
- 3-car side entry garage

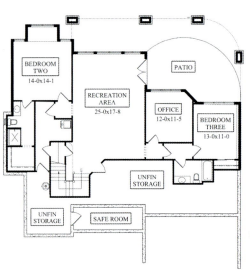

Optional
Lower Level
1,330 sq. ft.

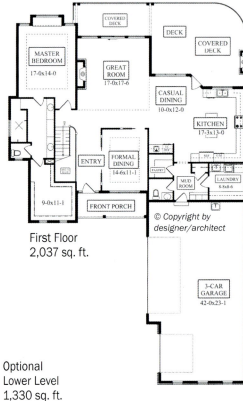

© Copyright by designer/architect

First Floor
2,037 sq. ft.

Images provided by designer/architect

Plan #F13-091D-0534

Dimensions: 76'10" W x 78'2" D
Heated Sq. Ft.: 3,952
Bedrooms: 4 **Bathrooms:** 4
Exterior Walls: 2" x 6"
Foundation: Crawl space standard; slab, basement, daylight basement or walk-out basement for an additional fee

See index for more information

Features

- Perfect symmetry creates a stunning and stylish Modern Farmhouse facade that is formidable as well as memorable with curb appeal

- The great room is topped with rustic beams creating a warm interior space and the stone fireplace adds to that cozy feel

- The kitchen features a large hidden prep kitchen, a huge island overlooking the great room, and a sizable walk-in pantry

- The master suite enjoys views of the covered rear porch with an outdoor fireplace, and also has a large walk-in closet and an elegant spa style bath

- A secluded pocket office is tucked away behind the kitchen

- 3-car side entry garage

Second Floor
1,530 sq. ft.

© Copyright by designer/architect

First Floor
2,422 sq. ft.

Images provided by designer/architect

Plan #F13-055D-1049

Dimensions: 85'6" W x 61'3" D
Heated Sq. Ft.: 2,470
Bonus Sq. Ft.: 602
Bedrooms: 4 **Bathrooms:** 2½
Foundation: Crawl space or slab
standard; basement or daylight
basement for an additional fee

See index for more information

Features

- Amazingly open, the beamed great room blends with the kitchen perfectly to form the main gathering space
- A large kitchen island overlooks the great room and has casual dining space
- The master bedroom is luxurious with its huge walk-in closet and posh bath featuring a corner whirlpool tub, a double-bowl vanity, and separate shower
- There are three additional bedrooms and each have their own walk-in closet and are in close proximity to a bath
- An outdoor living/grilling porch promises to be a favorite spot year-round thanks to the outdoor grill, vaulted ceiling and fireplace
- 2-car side entry garage, and a 1-car front entry garage

Images provided by designer/architect

First Floor
2,470 sq. ft.

© Copyright by
designer/architect

Optional
Second Floor
602 sq. ft.

Plan #F13-051D-0970

Dimensions: 37' W x 68' D
Heated Sq. Ft.: 1,354
Bedrooms: 2   **Bathrooms:** 2
Exterior Walls: 2" x 6"
Foundation: Basement standard; crawl space or slab for an additional fee

See index for more information

Features

- Small and stylish, this home offers the layout everyone loves in an easy-to-maintain size
- The covered front porch is large enough for relaxing, while the rear has a screened porch with access onto an open deck, perfect when grilling
- The master bedroom has a private bath with an oversized walk-in shower, a double-bowl vanity, and a spacious walk-in closet
- Bedroom 2 is just steps away from a full bath and on the opposite side of the house from the master bedroom for privacy
- 2-car front entry garage

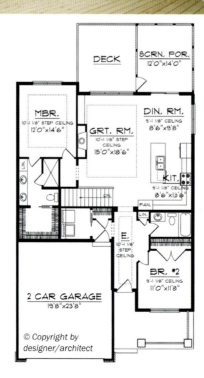

Images provided by designer/architect

© Copyright by designer/architect

Plan #F13-101D-0044

Images provided by designer/architect

Dimensions:	101'6" W x 82'8" D
Heated Sq. Ft.:	3,897
Bonus Sq. Ft.:	1,678
Bedrooms: 4	Bathrooms: 3½
Exterior Walls:	2" x 6"
Foundation:	Walk-out basement

See index for more information

Features

- No detail has been overlooked in this Craftsman-inspired luxury home
- The first floor offers a central gathering spot with the great room that has direct access to the open kitchen that features a huge island with food preparation space as well as casual dining
- The covered deck wraps the rear of the home and includes a spot off the master bedroom with a pergola above and an outdoor fireplace
- The garage includes a toy storage space that could be designated for children's toys, or adult toys like an ATV or sports equipment
- The optional lower level has an additional 1,678 square feet of living area and is comprised of a game area, a TV area, an exercise room, a wet bar, a guest bedroom with a full bath
- 2-car front entry garage, and a 1-car side entry garage

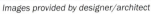

Second Floor
1,251 sq. ft.

© Copyright by designer/architect

First Floor
2,646 sq. ft.

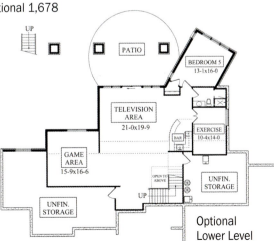

Optional
Lower Level
1,678 sq. ft.

Plan #F13-055D-0748

Images provided by designer/architect

Dimensions:	67'2" W x 55'10" D
Heated Sq. Ft.:	2,525
Bedrooms: 4	**Bathrooms:** 3

Foundation: Crawl space or slab standard; basement or daylight basement for an additional fee

See index for more information

Plan #F13-143D-0007

Images provided by designer/architect

Dimensions:	49'2" W x 47' D
Heated Sq. Ft.:	1,380
Bedrooms: 3	**Bathrooms:** 2
Exterior Walls:	2" x 6"

Foundation: Basement, crawl space or slab, please specify when ordering

See index for more information

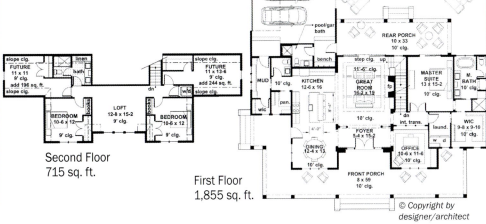

Plan #F13-091D-0529

Dimensions:	68'4" W x 76'2" D
Heated Sq. Ft.:	2,570
Bonus Sq. Ft.:	440
Bedrooms: 3	Bathrooms: 3½
Exterior Walls:	2" x 6"

Foundation: Basement standard; slab, crawl space, daylight basement or walk-out basement for an additional fee

See index for more information

Second Floor
715 sq. ft.

First Floor
1,855 sq. ft.

Plan #F13-028D-0118

Dimensions:	50' W x 44' D
Heated Sq. Ft.:	1,500
Bedrooms: 3	Bathrooms: 2
Exterior Walls:	2" x 6"

Foundation: Floating slab standard; monolithic slab, crawl space, basement or walk-out basement for an additional fee

See index for more information

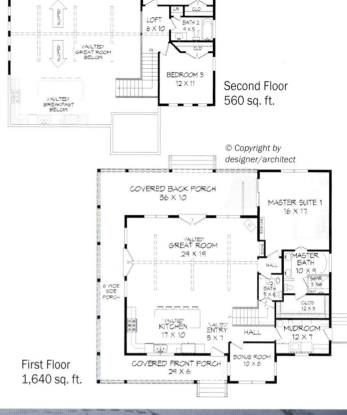

Second Floor
560 sq. ft.

© Copyright by
designer/architect

First Floor
1,640 sq. ft.

Plan #F13-141D-0100

Dimensions:	52'2" W x 46'6" D
Heated Sq. Ft.:	2,200
Bedrooms: 3	Bathrooms: 2½
Exterior Walls:	2" x 6"

Foundation: Crawl space or slab, please specify when ordering

See index for more information

Images provided by designer/architect

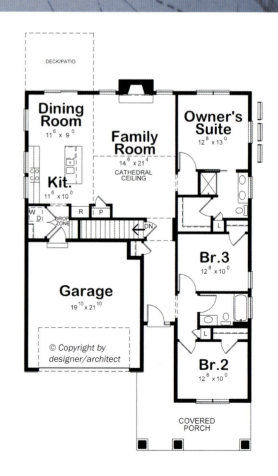

© Copyright by
designer/architect

Plan #F13-026D-2051

Dimensions:	40' W x 62' D
Heated Sq. Ft.:	1,511
Bedrooms: 3	Bathrooms: 2
Exterior Walls:	2" x 6"

Foundation: Basement standard; crawl space, slab or walk-out basement for an additional fee

See index for more information

Images provided by designer/architect

Plan #F13-167D-0004

Dimensions: 42'4" W x 53' D
Heated Sq. Ft.: 2,589
Bonus Sq. Ft.: 465
Bedrooms: 4   **Bathrooms:** 4
Exterior Walls: 2" x 6"
Foundation: Crawl space standard; slab for an additional fee

See index for more information

Optional Second Floor
465 sq. ft.

bonus room/artist's loft efficiency apt (opt.)
20'x17'

Detached Garage

garage 20'x20'6"
outdoor shower 6'6"x4'6"
pool bath 6'x5'

Second Floor
754 sq. ft.

storage 7'6"x11'9"
w.i.c. 7'6"x5'9"
hall 14' x 5'6"
bedroom 12' x 11'10"
bath
bedroom 12' x 12'9"
w.i.c. 5' x 10'

First Floor
1,835 sq. ft.

owner's suite 13' x 15'
keeping room 16' x 11'6"
owner's bath
great room 16' x 20'
storage
dining 12' x 13'6"
w.i.c. 7'6"x7'6"
bath
pantry 5'6" x 4'
foyer 5' x 12'6"
kitchen 15' x 14'6"
mudroom 5'9" x 8'6"
office/bedroom 12' x 11'9"

© Copyright by designer/architect

Images provided by designer/architect

Plan #F13-141D-0282

Dimensions: 32' W x 31' D
Heated Sq. Ft.: 1,359
Bonus Sq. Ft.: 200
Bedrooms: 2   **Bathrooms:** 2
Exterior Walls: 2" x 6"
Foundation: Slab

See index for more information

Images provided by designer/architect

Second Floor
992 sq. ft.

8' CLG CLOSET 8 x 10
SHWR 5 x 4
BATH 5 x 6
HALL
VAULTED KITCHEN 10 x 10
BEDROOM #1 12 x 16
VAULTED FAMILY ROOM 20 x 16
BALCONY 24 x 10

Optional Third Floor
200 sq. ft.

200 SF ART LOFT 11 x 16

First Floor
367 sq. ft.

BDRM #2 9 x 11
BATH #2 7 x 7
ENTRY 10 x 7
PORCH 7 x 14
STORAGE 10 x 19
10' CEILING DOUBLE GARAGE 21 x 19

© Copyright by designer/architect

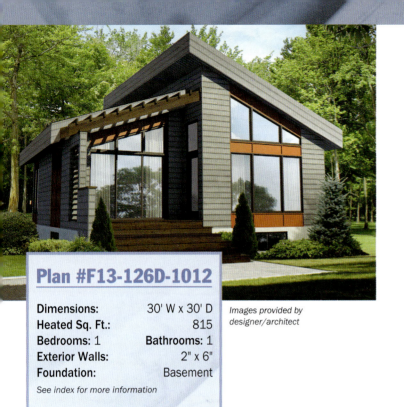

Plan #F13-126D-1012

Dimensions:	30' W x 30' D
Heated Sq. Ft.:	815
Bedrooms: 1	Bathrooms: 1
Exterior Walls:	2" x 6"
Foundation:	Basement

See index for more information

Images provided by designer/architect

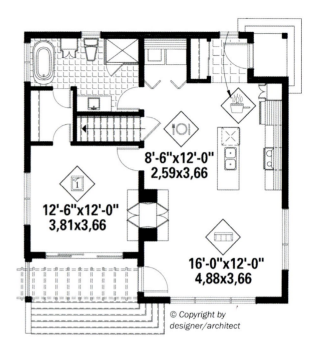

8'-6"x12'-0"
2,59x3,66

12'-6"x12'-0"
3,81x3,66

16'-0"x12'-0"
4,88x3,66

© Copyright by designer/architect

Plan #F13-130D-0337

Dimensions:	48' W x 63' D
Heated Sq. Ft.:	2,107
Bedrooms: 4	Bathrooms: 3½

Foundation: Slab standard; crawl space or basement for an additional fee

See index for more information

Images provided by designer/architect

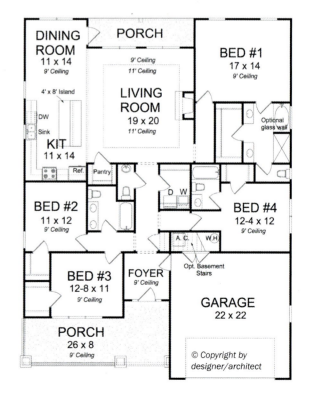

DINING ROOM
11 x 14
9' Ceiling

PORCH
9' Ceiling
11' Ceiling

BED #1
17 x 14
9' Ceiling

4' x 8' Island

LIVING ROOM
19 x 20
11' Ceiling

DW

Sink

KIT
11 x 14

Ref.   Pantry

Optional glass wall

BED #2
11 x 12
9' Ceiling

D   W

BED #4
12-4 x 12
9' Ceiling

A. C.   W.H.

BED #3
12-8 x 11
9' Ceiling

FOYER
9' Ceiling

Opt. Basement Stairs

GARAGE
22 x 22

PORCH
26 x 8
9' Ceiling

© Copyright by designer/architect

© Copyright by
designer/architect

Plan #F13-077D-0088

Dimensions:	30' W x 36' D
Heated Sq. Ft.:	800
Bedrooms: 2	**Bathrooms:** 1
Foundation:	Slab

See index for more information

Images provided by designer/architect

Plan #F13-084D-0090

Dimensions:	73'6" W x 61' D
Heated Sq. Ft.:	2,221
Bonus Sq. Ft.:	403
Bedrooms: 4	**Bathrooms:** 2

Foundation: Slab standard; crawl
space or basement for an
additional fee

See index for more information

*Images provided by
designer/architect*

Optional
Second Floor
403 sq. ft.

FUTURE
11-8 x 27-2
8' CEILING
SLOPED TO
5' SIDE WALLS

© Copyright by
designer/architect

First Floor
2,221 sq. ft.

Plan #F13-077D-0058

Dimensions: 64'6" W x 61'4" D
Heated Sq. Ft.: 2,002
Bedrooms: 3   **Bathrooms:** 2
Exterior Walls: 2" x 6"
Foundation: Slab, crawl space, basement or walk-out basement, please specify when ordering

See index for more information

Images provided by designer/architect

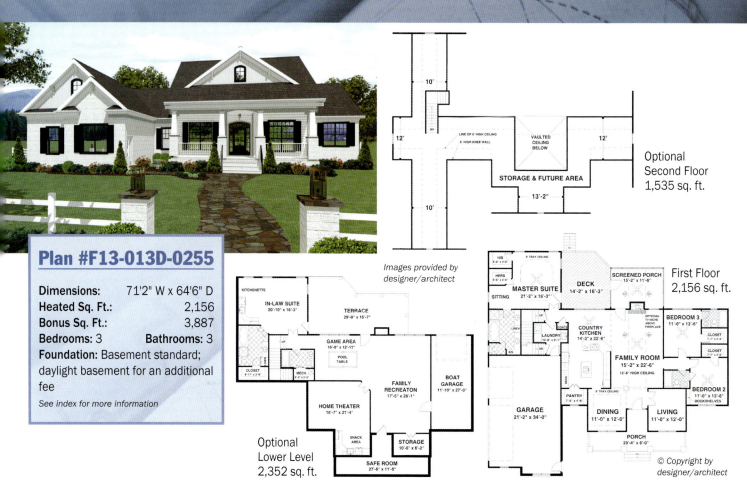

Plan #F13-013D-0255

Dimensions: 71'2" W x 64'6" D
Heated Sq. Ft.: 2,156
Bonus Sq. Ft.: 3,887
Bedrooms: 3   **Bathrooms:** 3
Foundation: Basement standard; daylight basement for an additional fee

See index for more information

Images provided by designer/architect

Optional Second Floor 1,535 sq. ft.

First Floor 2,156 sq. ft.

Optional Lower Level 2,352 sq. ft.

© Copyright by designer/architect

houseplansandmore.com

Plan #F13-007D-0135

Dimensions:	57' W x 36'4" D
Heated Sq. Ft.:	801
Bedrooms: 2	**Bathrooms:** 1
Foundation:	Slab

See index for more information

Images provided by designer/architect

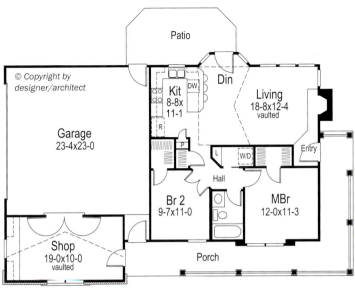

© Copyright by designer/architect

Patio

Garage
23-4x23-0

Kit
8-8x
11-1

Din

Living
18-8x12-4
vaulted

Entry

Hall

Br 2
9-7x11-0

MBr
12-0x11-3

Shop
19-0x10-0
vaulted

Porch

Plan #F13-011D-0657

Dimensions:	26' W x 34' D
Heated Sq. Ft.:	1,394
Bedrooms: 3	**Bathrooms:** 2½
Exterior Walls:	2" x 6"

Foundation: Crawl space or slab standard; basement for an additional fee

See index for more information

First Floor
714 sq. ft.

PATIO

12/8 X 12/8 +/-
(9' CLG.)

DINING
9/6 X 10/6 +/-
(9' CLG.)

REF

STOR

LIVING
15/0 X 14/6 +/-
(9' CLG.)

PAN

UP

COVERED
PORCH
22/0 X 6/0

Second Floor
680 sq. ft.

© Copyright by designer/architect

MASTER
13/0 X 12/8

DN

BR. 2
12/0 X 10/6 +/-

BR. 3
10/4 X 10/6

Images provided by designer/architect

Plan #F13-033D-0012

Dimensions:	60' W x 43' D
Heated Sq. Ft.:	1,546
Bedrooms: 3	**Bathrooms:** 2
Foundation:	Basement

See index for more information

Images provided by designer/architect

© Copyright by designer/architect

Plan #F13-086D-0151

Dimensions:	55' W x 55' D
Heated Sq. Ft.:	3,528
Bedrooms: 4	**Bathrooms:** 3½

Foundation: Basement standard; walk-out basement for an additional fee

See index for more information

Images provided by designer/architect

First Floor
1,838 sq. ft.

Lower Level
1,690 sq. ft.

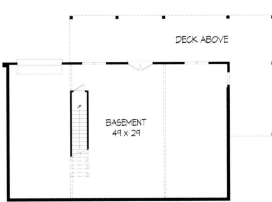

First Floor
1,500 sq. ft.

Plan #F13-141D-0333

Dimensions: 60' W x 50' D
Heated Sq. Ft.: 1,500
Bonus Sq. Ft.: 1,500
Bedrooms: 2   **Bathrooms:** 2½
Foundation: Walk-out basement standard; crawl space or slab for an additional fee

See index for more information

Images provided by designer/architect

Optional Lower Level
1,500 sq. ft.

Second Floor
938 sq. ft.

Images provided by designer/architect

Plan #F13-172D-0046

Dimensions: 42' W x 40' D
Heated Sq. Ft.: 1,827
Bonus Sq. Ft.: 992
Bedrooms: 3   **Bathrooms:** 2½
Exterior Walls: 2" x 6"
Foundation: Basement standard; crawl space, monolithic slab, stem wall slab, daylight basement or walk-out basement for an additional fee

See index for more information

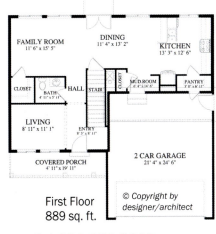

Optional Lower Level
992 sq. ft.

First Floor
889 sq. ft.

© Copyright by designer/architect

Second Floor
605 sq. ft.

MASTER
BEDROOM
10⁴ x 12¹⁰

DN

W&D

BEDROOM
3
9⁸ x 10⁸

MSTR.
BATH

BEDROOM
2
10⁰ x 11⁰

BATH
2

© Copyright by
designer/architect

Plan #F13-111D-0042

Dimensions: 29' W x 30' D
Heated Sq. Ft.: 1,074
Bedrooms: 3   Bathrooms: 2½
Foundation: Slab standard; crawl
space for an additional fee

See index for more information

KITCHEN
9⁰ x 10⁰

PWDR

UP

PATIO

DINING &
LIVING
14⁰ x 19⁰

GARAGE
10⁰ x 19⁸

PORCH

First Floor
469 sq. ft.

Images provided by designer/architect

Plan #F13-155D-0031

Dimensions: 78'10" W x 110'6" D
Heated Sq. Ft.: 3,437
Bonus Sq. Ft.: 1,148
Bedrooms: 6   Bathrooms: 4
Foundation: Crawl space or slab
standard; basement for an
additional fee

See index for more information

*Images provided by
designer/architect*

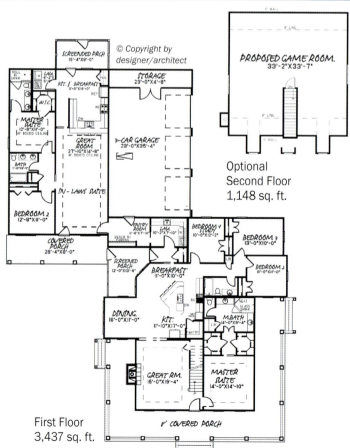

© Copyright by
designer/architect

PROPOSED GAME ROOM
33'-2" X 33'-7"

Optional
Second Floor
1,148 sq. ft.

First Floor
3,437 sq. ft.

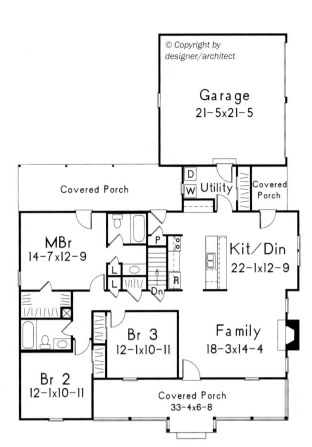

Plan #F13-001D-0031

Dimensions: 48' W x 66' D
Heated Sq. Ft.: 1,501
Bedrooms: 3   **Bathrooms:** 2
Foundation: Basement standard; crawl space or slab for an additional fee

See index for more information

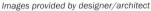

Images provided by designer/architect

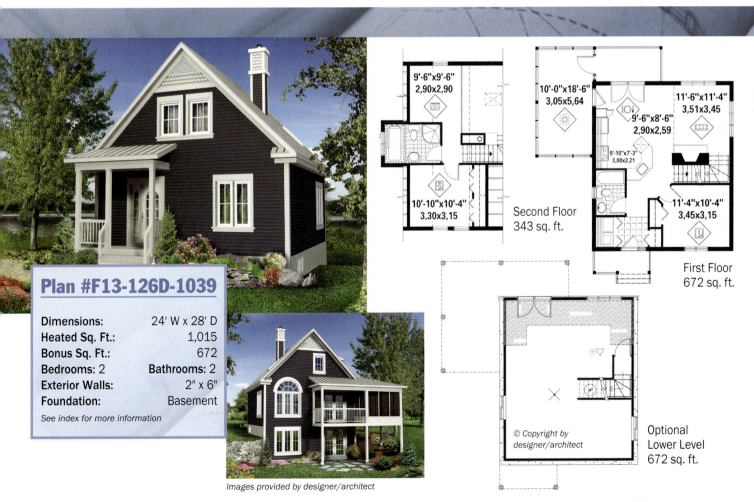

Plan #F13-126D-1039

Dimensions: 24' W x 28' D
Heated Sq. Ft.: 1,015
Bonus Sq. Ft.: 672
Bedrooms: 2   **Bathrooms:** 2
Exterior Walls: 2" x 6"
Foundation: Basement

See index for more information

Images provided by designer/architect

Plan #F13-076D-0220

Dimensions:	97'2" W x 87'7" D
Heated Sq. Ft.:	3,061
Bonus Sq. Ft.:	3,644
Bedrooms: 3	**Bathrooms** 3½

Foundation: Basement standard; crawl space or slab for an additional fee

See index for more information

Features

- This luxury Craftsman home is loaded with curb appeal thanks to multiple gables, and a covered porch adding that undeniable charm
- The first floor is open and airy with the main gathering spaces combining perfectly maximizing the square footage
- The kitchen is open to the family room with a grilling terrace nearby
- The optional lower level has an additional 2,975 square feet of living area including a hobby room, theater, office, and a recreation area with a bar
- The optional second floor has an additional 669 square feet of living area with 277 square feet in the bedroom and 392 square feet in the recreation area
- 3-car front entry garage

© Copyright by designer/architect

Images provided by designer/architect

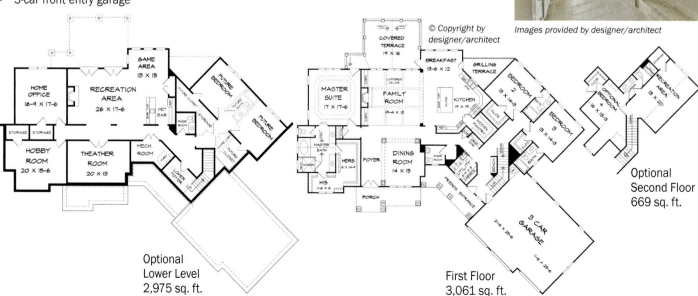

Optional Lower Level
2,975 sq. ft.

First Floor
3,061 sq. ft.

Optional Second Floor
669 sq. ft.

Plan #F13-055D-0894

Dimensions: 45' W x 62'4" D
Heated Sq. Ft.: 1,572
Bonus Sq. Ft.: 276
Bedrooms: 3 **Bathrooms:** 2
Foundation: Crawl space or slab standard; basement or daylight basement for an additional fee

See index for more information

Features

- Charming European style dictates the exterior, while an open and inviting floor plan dominates the interior
- The open great room with fireplace flows into the hearth/dining area that accesses the rear covered grilling porch
- An amazing master bath boasts a double-bowl vanity, and a whirlpool tub/shower with flanking walk-in closets
- The bonus room above the garage has an additional 276 square feet of living area perfect for a children's play area, home office, or even a media room
- 2-car front entry garage

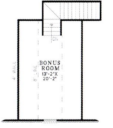

Optional
Second Floor
276 sq. ft.

First Floor
1,572 sq. ft.

© Copyright by
designer/architect

Images provided by designer/architect

Plan #F13-032D-1135

Dimensions:	65' W x 50' D
Heated Sq. Ft.:	1,788
Bonus Sq. Ft.:	1,788
Bedrooms: 2	**Bathrooms:** 2
Exterior Walls:	2" x 6"

Foundation: Basement standard; crawl space, floating slab or monolithic slab for an additional fee

See index for more information

Images provided by designer/architect

Features

- Stylish one-level living is open, modern and feels relaxing
- Directly off the foyer is the office/den, perfect for easy access with business associates
- The master suite enjoys double walk-in closets that lead to a posh private bath
- The kitchen has an open feel to the nearby dining room and beyond to the living room featuring a cozy fireplace
- A handy mud room connects the garage to the rest of the home
- The optional lower level has an additional 1,788 square feet of living area
- 2-car front entry garage

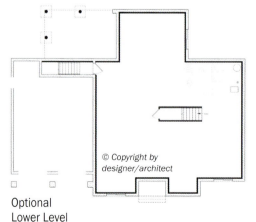

© Copyright by designer/architect

Optional
Lower Level
1,788 sq. ft.

First Floor
1,788 sq. ft.

Plan #F13-163D-0003

Dimensions:	56' W x 40' D
Heated Sq. Ft.:	1,416
Bedrooms: 3	Bathrooms: 2
Exterior Walls:	2" x 6"
Foundation:	Crawl space

See index for more information

Images provided by designer/architect

Features

- Covered front and back porches are large enough to enjoy the outdoors in comfort
- The great room is open to both the kitchen and dining area on the left side of the house for an open, airy feel
- All three bedrooms are located on the right side of the house with the master suite having a private sitting porch
- The laundry room is conveniently located just off of the kitchen

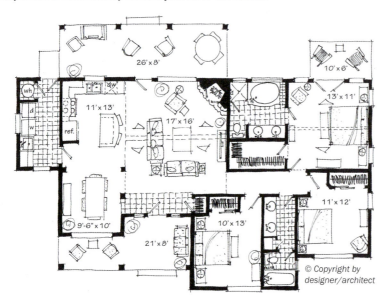

© Copyright by designer/architect

Plan #F13-101D-0056

Dimensions:	72' W x 77' D
Heated Sq. Ft.:	2,593
Bonus Sq. Ft.:	1,892
Bedrooms: 2	Bathrooms: 2½
Exterior Walls:	2" x 6"
Foundation:	Walk-out basement

See index for more information

Features

- This stunning home has the look and feel homeowners love with its sleek interior and open floor plan
- The great room, kitchen and dining area combine maximizing the square footage and making these spaces functional and comfortable
- The master bedroom enjoys a first floor location adding convenience for the homeowners
- The optional lower level has an additional 1,892 square feet of living area and adds extra amenities like a media area, billiards space, recreation and exercise rooms
- 3-car front entry garage

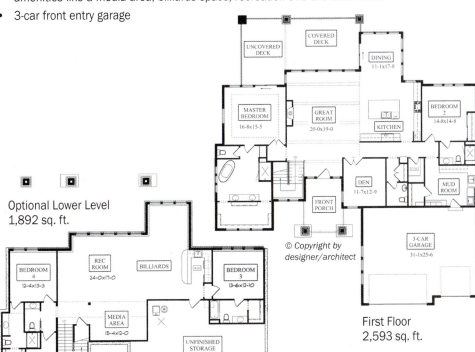

Optional Lower Level
1,892 sq. ft.

© Copyright by designer/architect

First Floor
2,593 sq. ft.

Images provided by designer/architect

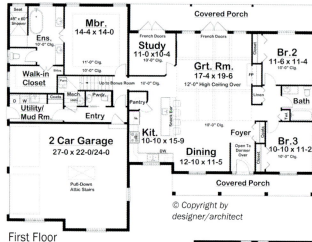

First Floor
2,148 sq. ft.

© Copyright by designer/architect

Plan #F13-144D-0039

Dimensions:	71' W x 49' D
Heated Sq. Ft.:	2,148
Bonus Sq. Ft.:	707
Bedrooms: 3	Bathrooms: 2½
Exterior Walls:	2" x 6"

Foundation: Crawl space standard; slab, basement, daylight basement or walk-out basement for an additional fee

See index for more information

Images provided by designer/architect

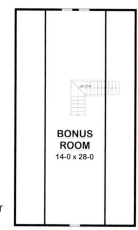

Optional
Second Floor
707 sq. ft.

BONUS ROOM
14-0 x 28-0

Plan #F13-156D-0002

Dimensions:	24' W x 27'6" D
Heated Sq. Ft.:	576
Bedrooms: 1	Bathrooms: 1

Foundation: Slab standard; crawl space for an additional fee

See index for more information

© Copyright by designer/architect

Images provided by designer/architect

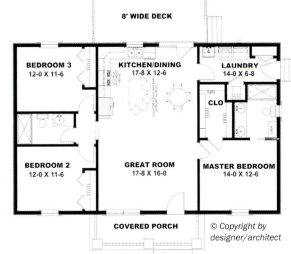

Plan #F13-028D-0100

Dimensions:	46' W x 42'6" D
Heated Sq. Ft.:	1,311
Bedrooms: 3	Bathrooms: 2
Exterior Walls:	2" x 6"

Foundation: Floating slab standard; monolithic slab, crawl space, basement or walk-out basement for an additional fee

See index for more information

Images provided by designer/architect

8' WIDE DECK

BEDROOM 3
12-0 X 11-6

KITCHEN/DINING
17-8 X 12-6

LAUNDRY
14-0 X 6-8

CLO

BEDROOM 2
12-0 X 11-6

GREAT ROOM
17-8 X 16-0

MASTER BEDROOM
14-0 X 12-6

COVERED PORCH

© Copyright by designer/architect

Plan #F13-076D-0306

Dimensions:	89'9" W x 76'4" D
Heated Sq. Ft.:	2,000
Bonus Sq. Ft.:	508
Bedrooms: 3	Bathrooms: 2½
Foundation:	Slab

See index for more information

Images provided by designer/architect

© Copyright by designer/architect

COVERED TERRACE
18-3 X 14

MASTER SUITE
13-6 X 14-6

KITCHEN
11-6 X 16-6

FAMILY ROOM
18-3 X 16-6

BEDROOM 3
13 X 12

MASTER BATH

PANTRY
7-6 X 4-6

DINING ROOM
14-6 X 13

FOYER
7-3 X 13

BATH

CLOSET
8-6 X 9-6

PORCH

BEDROOM 2
13 X 12

2 CAR GARAGE
26-6 X 22-6

First Floor
2,000 sq. ft.

BONUS ROOM
21-6 X 22-6

Optional Second Floor
508 sq. ft.

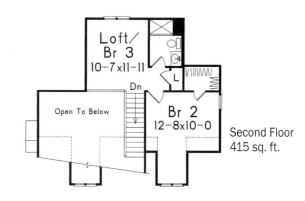

Loft/Br 3
10-7x11-11

Open To Below

Dn

Br 2
12-8x10-0

Second Floor
415 sq. ft.

Plan #F13-058D-0020

Dimensions:	46' W x 42'6" D
Heated Sq. Ft.:	1,428
Bedrooms: 3	Bathrooms: 2
Foundation:	Basement

See index for more information

Images provided by designer/architect

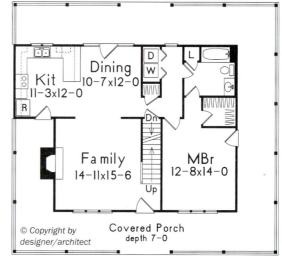

Kit
11-3x12-0

Dining
10-7x12-0

D W

Dn

Family
14-11x15-6

MBr
12-8x14-0

Up

R

© Copyright by designer/architect

Covered Porch
depth 7-0

First Floor
1,013 sq. ft.

CVRD. PORCH
16'0"x10'4"

GRT. RM.
vaulted ceiling
17'8"x14'6"

MBR.
10'-1 1/8" step ceiling
14'0"x12'0"

BR. #3
9'-1 1/8" ceiling
10'0"x11'0"

DIN.
vaulted ceiling
14'0"x11'6"

KIT.
vaulted ceiling
10'6"x12'4"

BR. #2
9'-1 1/8" ceiling
11'0"x11'0"

E.
vaulted ceiling

3 CAR GARAGE
29'4"x21'8"

© Copyright by designer/architect

Plan #F13-051D-0757

Dimensions:	55' W x 51'8" D
Heated Sq. Ft.:	1,501
Bedrooms: 3	Bathrooms: 2
Exterior Walls:	2" x 6"

Foundation: Basement standard; crawl space or slab for an additional fee

See index for more information

Images provided by designer/architect

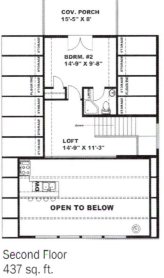

Plan #F13-088D-0841

Dimensions:	32' W x 68' D
Heated Sq. Ft.:	1,599
Bedrooms: 2	Bathrooms: 2
Exterior Walls:	2" x 6"
Foundation:	Piers

See index for more information

Images provided by designer/architect

Second Floor
437 sq. ft.

First Floor
1,162 sq. ft.

COV. PORCH
15'-5" X 8'

BDRM. #2
14'-9" X 9'-8"

LOFT
14'-9" X 11'-3"

OPEN TO BELOW

COV. ENTRY PORCH
15'-5" X 8'

MASTER SUITE
11' X 14'

WIC

UTILITY

KITCHEN
11'-4" X 11'-8"

LIVING
15'-1" X 23'-4"

DINING
11'-4" X 8'-8"

OPEN PORCH
28'-8" X 20'

© Copyright by designer/architect

Plan #F13-007D-0196

Dimensions:	27' W x 27' D
Heated Sq. Ft.:	421
Bedrooms: 1	Bathrooms: 1
Foundation:	Slab

See index for more information

Images provided by designer/architect

Bedroom
12-0x8-6

Garage
12-0x20-4

Liv. Rm./Kit.
14-0x12-1

Entry

Porch

© Copyright by designer/architect

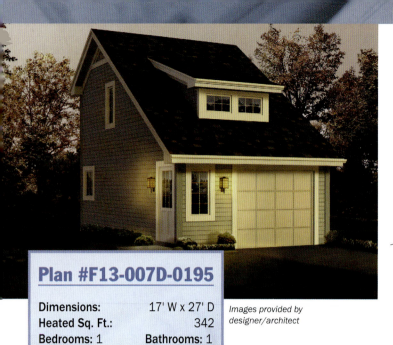

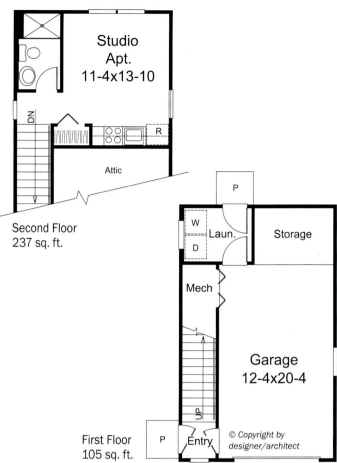

Studio Apt.
11-4x13-10

DN

Attic

Second Floor
237 sq. ft.

P

W
D

Laun.

Storage

Mech

R

Garage
12-4x20-4

UP

P

Entry

© Copyright by
designer/architect

First Floor
105 sq. ft.

Plan #F13-007D-0195

Images provided by designer/architect

Dimensions:	17' W x 27' D
Heated Sq. Ft.:	342
Bedrooms: 1	**Bathrooms:** 1
Foundation:	Slab

See index for more information

Layout for
Slab and
Crawl Space
Foundation

D
W

W/H

FURN

© Copyright by designer/architect

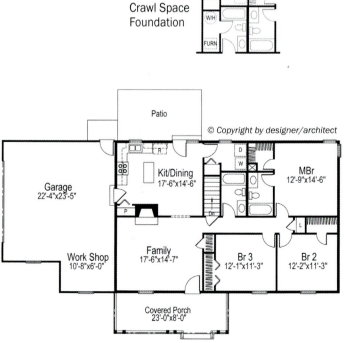

Patio

Garage
22'-4"x23'-5"

Kit/Dining
17'-6"x14'-6"

D
W

MBr
12'-9"x14'-6"

P

DN

Work Shop
10'-8"x6'-0"

Family
17'-6"x14'-7"

Br 3
12'-1"x11'-3"

Br 2
12'-2"x11'-3"

L

Covered Porch
23'-0"x8'-0"

Plan #F13-001D-0024

Images provided by designer/architect

Dimensions:	68' W x 38' D
Heated Sq. Ft.:	1,360
Bedrooms: 3	**Bathrooms:** 2

Foundation: Basement standard; crawl space or slab for an additional fee

See index for more information

Plan #F13-001D-0085

Dimensions:	28' W x 38' D
Heated Sq. Ft.:	720
Bedrooms: 2	**Bathrooms:** 1
Foundation: Crawl space standard; slab for an additional fee	

See index for more information

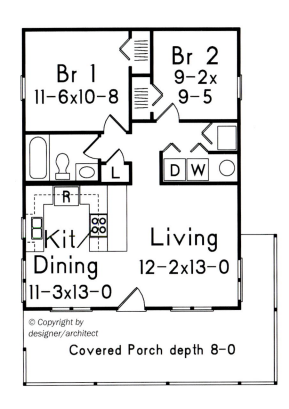

Images provided by designer/architect

Br 1
11-6x10-8

Br 2
9-2x
9-5

D W

Kit/
Dining
11-3x13-0

Living
12-2x13-0

© Copyright by designer/architect

Covered Porch depth 8-0

Plan #F13-007D-0145

Dimensions:	40' W x 38' D
Heated Sq. Ft.:	1,005
Bedrooms: 2	**Bathrooms:** 1½
Foundation:	Slab

See index for more information

Images provided by designer/architect

MBr
12-0x12-4

Br 2
9-7x11-0

Hall

Garage Below

Second Floor
492 sq. ft.

Patio

Din

Living Rm.
18-6x12-8

Kit
8-8x
8-8

DW

Entry

Porch

W/D

© Copyright by designer/architect

3-Car Garage
34-0x22-4

First Floor
513 sq. ft.

Plan #F13-123D-0117

Dimensions: 57'4" W x 58'6" D
Heated Sq. Ft.: 2,499
Bedrooms: 4 **Bathrooms:** 2½
Foundation: Basement standard; crawl space, slab or walk-out basement for an additional fee

See index for more information

Images provided by designer/architect

Second Floor
864 sq. ft.

First Floor
1,635 sq. ft.

Br. 2
11⁰ x 11¹⁰

Br. 3
11⁸ x 11⁸

Loft
10⁸ x 11

Br. 4
11⁸ x 12⁴

9'-0" Ceiling

Bench

Balcony

DN

Covered Patio

Bench

Mbr.
13 x 13⁶
10'-0" Ceiling

Grt. Rm.
16 x 14¹⁰
10'-0" Ceiling

Bfst.
9 x 9

K.
14 x 12⁸

W D

Mud Room

Pantry

Gar.
22⁴ x 24⁰

Bench/Lockers

DN   UP

Flex
14 x 11

Covered Porch

© Copyright by designer/architect

Plan #F13-007D-0164

Dimensions: 53' W x 55' D
Heated Sq. Ft.: 1,741
Bedrooms: 4 **Bathrooms:** 2
Foundation: Crawl space standard; slab or basement for an additional fee

See index for more information

Images provided by designer/architect

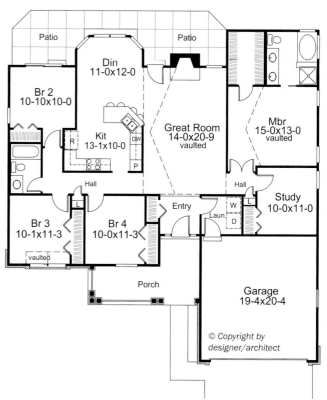

Patio

Patio

Din
11-0x12-0

Br 2
10-10x10-0

Kit
13-1x10-0

Great Room
14-0x20-9
vaulted

Mbr
15-0x13-0
vaulted

Hall

Hall

Br 3
10-1x11-3

Br 4
10-0x11-3

Entry

Laun

Study
10-0x11-0

vaulted

Porch

Garage
19-4x20-4

© Copyright by designer/architect

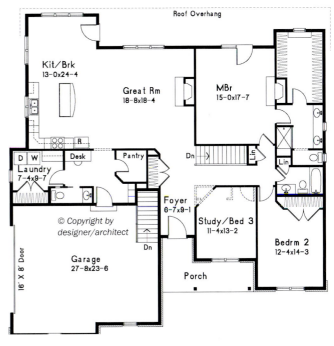

Plan #F13-058D-0266

Dimensions:	60'8" W x 59'8" D
Heated Sq. Ft.:	2,176
Bedrooms: 3	Bathrooms: 2½
Exterior Walls:	2" x 6"
Foundation:	Basement

See index for more information

Images provided by designer/architect

© Copyright by designer/architect

Plan #F13-076D-0314

Dimensions:	84'11" W x 62'4" D
Heated Sq. Ft.:	2,981
Bedrooms: 3	Bathrooms: 3½
Foundation:	Slab

See index for more information

Images provided by designer/architect

Second Floor
746 sq. ft.

© Copyright by designer/architect

First Floor
2,235 sq. ft.

Plan #F13-130D-0338

Dimensions: 56' W x 63' D
Heated Sq. Ft.: 2,425
Bedrooms: 4   **Bathrooms:** 3½
Foundation: Slab standard; crawl space or basement for an additional fee

See index for more information

Images provided by designer/architect

Floor plan labels:
DINING ROOM 11 x 14, 9' Ceiling
PORCH
LIVING ROOM 19 x 20, 11' Ceiling
BED #1 14 x 17, 9' Ceiling
glass doors
4' x 8' Island
DW Sink
Eating Bar
KIT 11 x 14
Ref.
Pantry
BED #4 14 x 11, 9' Ceiling
W D Sink
BED #2 11 x 12, 9' Ceiling
GAME ROOM (Optional Suite) 18 x 12, 9' Ceiling
A.C. W.H.
Opt. Basement Stairs
BED #3 12-8 x 11, 9' Ceiling
FOYER 9' Ceiling
3 CAR GARAGE 30 x 22
PORCH 13-4 x 10-8, 9' Ceiling

© Copyright by designer/architect

Plan #F13-007D-0040

Dimensions: 28' W x 26' D
Heated Sq. Ft.: 632
Bedrooms: 1   **Bathrooms:** 1
Foundation: Slab

See index for more information

Images provided by designer/architect

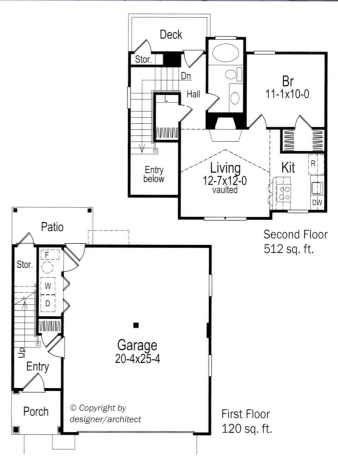

Second Floor 512 sq. ft.

Floor plan labels:
Deck
Stor.
Dn
Hall
Br 11-1x10-0
Living 12-7x12-0 vaulted
Kit
DW
Entry below

Patio
Stor.
F
W D
Up
Entry
Garage 20-4x25-4
Porch

© Copyright by designer/architect

First Floor 120 sq. ft.

Images provided by designer/architect

PORCH 8'-0" DEEP

KITCHEN/ DINING 12-0 X 16-6

BEDROOM 2 14-0 X 10-0

BATH 7-0 X 10-0

GREAT ROOM 20-0 X 14-0

VENTLESS OAK FIREPLACE

BEDROOM 1 13-0 X 10-0

© Copyright by designer/architect

PORCH 8'-0" DEEP

Plan #F13-028D-0108

Dimensions:	33' W x 40' D
Heated Sq. Ft.:	890
Bedrooms: 2	Bathrooms: 1
Exterior Walls:	2" x 6"

Foundation: Floating slab standard; monolithic slab, crawl space, basement or walk-out basement for an additional fee

See index for more information

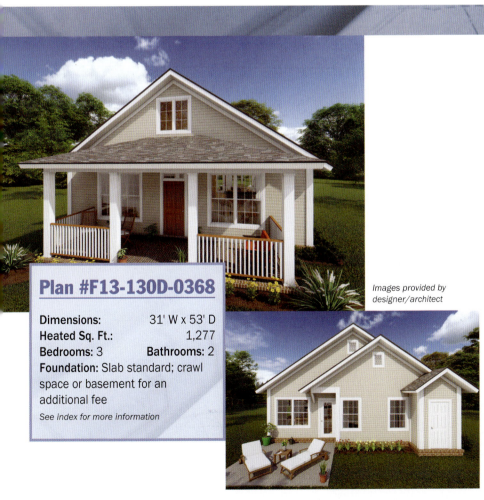

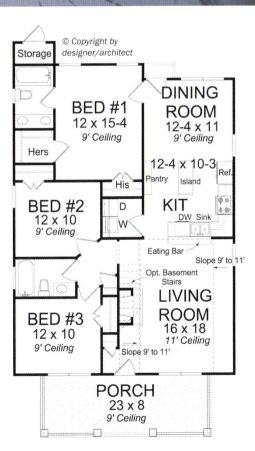

Images provided by designer/architect

Storage

© Copyright by designer/architect

BED #1 12 x 15-4 9' Ceiling

DINING ROOM 12-4 x 11 9' Ceiling

Hers

His

12-4 x 10-3

Pantry   Island   Ref.

BED #2 12 x 10 9' Ceiling

KIT

D

W

DW   Sink

Eating Bar

Slope 9' to 11'

Opt. Basement Stairs

BED #3 12 x 10 9' Ceiling

LIVING ROOM 16 x 18 11' Ceiling

Slope 9' to 11'

PORCH 23 x 8 9' Ceiling

Plan #F13-130D-0368

Dimensions:	31' W x 53' D
Heated Sq. Ft.:	1,277
Bedrooms: 3	Bathrooms: 2

Foundation: Slab standard; crawl space or basement for an additional fee

See index for more information

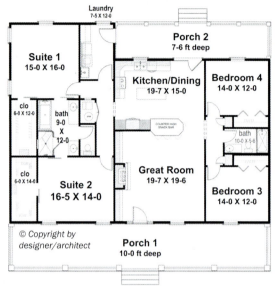

Images provided by designer/architect

Plan #F13-028D-0120

Dimensions: 56' W x 52' D
Heated Sq. Ft.: 2,096
Bedrooms: 4   **Bathrooms:** 2
Exterior Walls: 2" x 6"
Foundation: Floating slab standard; monolithic slab, crawl space, basement or walk-out basement for an additional fee

See index for more information

Laundry
7-5 X 12-0

Suite 1
15-0 X 16-0

clo
6-0 X 12-0

bath
9-0 X 12-0

clo
6-0 X 14-0

Suite 2
16-5 X 14-0

Porch 2
7-6 ft deep

Kitchen/Dining
19-7 X 15-0

COUNTER HIGH SNACK BAR

Bedroom 4
14-0 X 12-0

bath
10-0 X 5-6

Great Room
19-7 X 19-6

Bedroom 3
14-0 X 12-0

Porch 1
10-0 ft deep

© Copyright by designer/architect

Plan #F13-028D-0125

Dimensions: 50' W x 54' D
Heated Sq. Ft.: 1,860
Bedrooms: 3   **Bathrooms:** 2
Foundation: Floating slab standard; monolithic slab, crawl space, basement or walk-out basement for an additional fee

See index for more information

Images provided by designer/architect

LAUNDRY/MUDROOM
15'-8" x 14'-4"

PANTRY
10'-8" x 5'-4"

MASTER BATH
15'-8" x 9'-8"

CLO
5'-2" x 6'-0"

CLO
6'-6" x 6'-0"

CUSTOM SHOWER

MASTER BEDROOM
15'-8" x 14'-0"

COVERED PORCH
34'-0" x 10'-0"

KITCHEN/DINING
20'-0" x 15'-0"

BEDROOM NO. 3
12'-2" x 12'-0"

BATH NO. 2
10'-4" x 8'-0"

GREAT ROOM
20'-0" x 19'-0"

BEDROOM NO. 2
14'-4" x 11'-10"

COVERED PORCH
50'-0" x 10'-0"

© Copyright by designer/architect

Plan #F13-007D-0124

Dimensions: 65' W x 51' D
Heated Sq. Ft.: 1,944
Bedrooms: 3   **Bathrooms:** 2
Foundation: Basement standard; crawl space or slab for an additional fee

See index for more information

Images provided by designer/architect

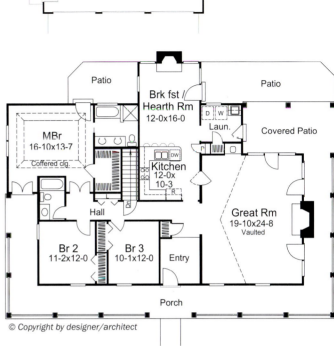

Plan #F13-056D-0133

Dimensions: 91'8" W x 69'8" D
Heated Sq. Ft.: 2,510
Bonus Sq. Ft.: 2,172
Bedrooms: 3   **Bathrooms:** 2½
Foundation: Basement standard; crawl space or slab for an additional fee

See index for more information

First Floor
2,510 sq. ft.

Optional
Lower Level
2,172 sq. ft.

Images provided by designer/architect

Detached Garage
23-4x23-4

© Copyright by
designer/architect

Patio

MBr
13-8x15-0
Std Coffer
Opt Vault

Kit
10-7x
13-4
Vaulted

Dining/ Brkfst
13-6x13-4
Vaulted

Br 2
10-0x10-6

Great Rm
17-8x17-8
Vaulted

Entry

Porch

Br 3
13-8x11-8

Plan #F13-121D-0016

Dimensions: 42'4" W x 54' D
Heated Sq. Ft.:   1,582
Bedrooms: 3   Bathrooms: 2
Foundation: Basement standard;
crawl space or slab for an
additional fee

See index for more information

Images provided by designer/architect

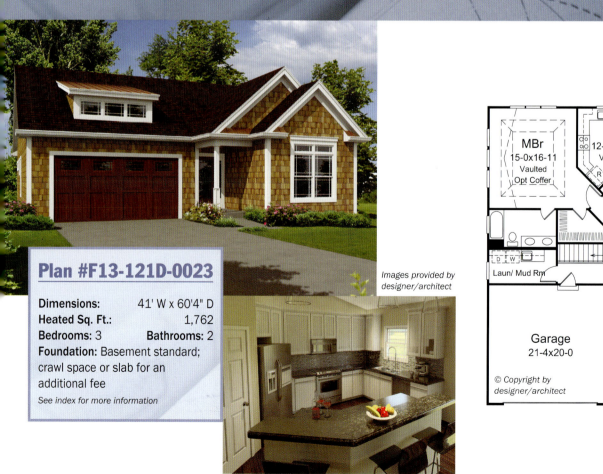

Patio

MBr
15-0x16-11
Vaulted
Opt Coffer

Kit
12-8x14-9
Vaulted

Dining
12-4x12-9
Vaulted

Great Rm
18-8x16-11
Vaulted

Laun/ Mud Rm

Garage
21-4x20-0

Entry

Br 2
10-11x12-2

Br 3
10-11x11-9

Porch

© Copyright by
designer/architect

*Images provided by
designer/architect*

Plan #F13-121D-0023

Dimensions: 41' W x 60'4" D
Heated Sq. Ft.:   1,762
Bedrooms: 3   Bathrooms: 2
Foundation: Basement standard;
crawl space or slab for an
additional fee

See index for more information

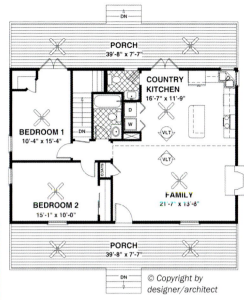

PORCH
39'-8" x 7'-7"

COUNTRY KITCHEN
16'-7" x 11'-9"

BEDROOM 1
10'-4" x 15'-4"

BEDROOM 2
15'-1" x 10'-0"

FAMILY
21'-7" x 13'-8"

PORCH
39'-8" x 7'-7"

© Copyright by designer/architect

Plan #F13-013D-0257

Dimensions: 40'3" W x 42'4" D
Heated Sq. Ft.: 1,059
Bedrooms: 2   **Bathrooms:** 1½
Foundation: Basement standard; crawl space or slab for an additional fee

See index for more information

Images provided by designer/architect

Mbr.
14 x 16
10'-0" Ceiling

Covered Patio

Br.2
11 x 11

Din.
10 x 20
Cath. Ceiling

Fam.
13 x 20
Cath. Ceiling

Br.3
11 x 11

K.
11 x 20
Cath. Ceiling

Entry

Pantry

Covered Porch

Office
12 x 10
Cath. Ceiling

Mud Room

Bonus
11 x 18

First Floor
2,278 sq. ft.

Gar.
26 x 23

Optional Second Floor
430 sq. ft.

Br.4
12 x 13

Rec.
13 x 18

Liv.
18 x 18

Thtr.
14 x 15

Bar
10 x 7

Exer.
14 x 11

Stor.

Stor.

© Copyright by designer/architect

Optional Lower Level
1,637 sq. ft.

Plan #F13-123D-0141

Dimensions: 73' W x 68'4" D
Heated Sq. Ft.: 2,278
Bonus Sq. Ft.: 2,067
Bedrooms: 3   **Bathrooms:** 2½
Foundation: Basement standard; crawl space, slab or walk-out basement for an additional fee

See index for more information

Images provided by designer/architect

Plan #F13-032D-0887

Dimensions:	42' W x 40' D
Heated Sq. Ft.:	1,212
Bonus Sq. Ft.:	1,212
Bedrooms: 2	Bathrooms: 1
Exterior Walls:	2" x 6"

Foundation: Basement standard; crawl space, floating slab or monolithic slab for an additional fee

See index for more information

Features

- This highly efficient home offers an open floor plan with beamed ceilings above adding a tremendous amount of architectural interest to the interior
- A fireplace acts like a partition between the bedrooms and the gathering spaces
- The large covered porch is a wonderful extension of the interior living spaces
- The island in the kitchen includes casual dining space and a double basin sink and dishwasher
- The optional lower level has an additional 1,212 square feet of living area

First Floor
1,212 sq. ft.

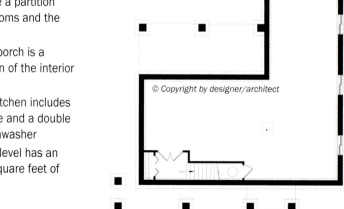

© Copyright by designer/architect

Optional Lower Level
1,212 sq. ft.

Images provided by designer/architect

houseplansandmore.com

Plan #F13-170D-0004

Dimensions: 48'4" W x 66'4" D
Heated Sq. Ft.: 1,581
Bedrooms: 3 **Bathrooms:** 2
Foundation: Slab or monolithic slab standard; crawl space, basement or daylight basement for an additional fee

See index for more information

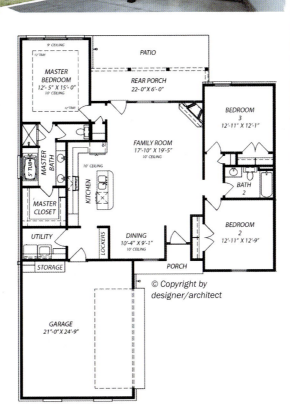

Features

- This modest sized one-story home offers many great features for today's family
- A side entry garage gives the exterior added curb appeal
- When entering from the garage you'll find lockers on the right and a utility room on the left
- The kitchen has a very open feel and includes an island with dining space
- The family room enjoys a cozy corner fireplace and an entire wall of windows that overlook the rear covered porch and beyond onto the patio
- The master bedroom and bath include a large walk-in closet
- Two secondary bedrooms share the full bath between them
- 2-car side entry garage

Images provided by designer/architect

© Copyright by designer/architect

Plan #F13-101D-0080

Dimensions:	79' W x 97'9" D
Heated Sq. Ft.:	2,682
Bonus Sq. Ft.:	1,940
Bedrooms: 2	**Bathrooms:** 2½
Exterior Walls:	2" x 6"

Foundation: Basement, daylight basement or walk-out basement, please specify when ordering

See index for more information

Features

- This rambling ranch home typifies the best in design with unique architectural features and today's most sought after Modern Farmhouse style exterior
- Enjoy the outdoors with outdoor living options including a patio, an uncovered deck, two covered decks and one with an outdoor fireplace
- The open kitchen has a large island overlooking the great room
- The private den has deck access, great as a home office
- The optional lower level has an additional 1,940 square feet of living area including three additional bedrooms, two baths, a laundry room, and rec room
- 3-car side entry garage

First Floor
2,682 sq. ft.

© Copyright by designer/architect

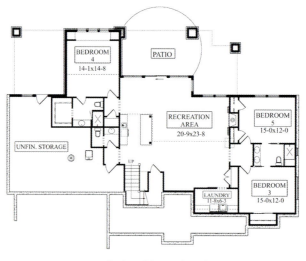

Optional Lower Level
1,940 sq. ft.

Images provided by designer/architect

Plan #F13-155D-0070

Dimensions: 60' W x 80'8" D
Heated Sq. Ft.: 2,464
Bonus Sq. Ft.: 758
Bedrooms: 4 **Bathrooms:** 3½
Foundation: Crawl space or slab standard; basement or daylight basement for an additional fee

See index for more information

Features

- The best in Farmhouse living, this home has a welcoming covered front porch and a rear grilling porch
- Decorative columns accent the private dining room, perfect for special events
- The combining of the great room, kitchen and breakfast room create a space that no doubt will be the central hub of this home
- The master suite offers all the amenities a homeowner needs including a private bath and walk-in closet
- The private bedroom 4 has its own bath and built-in desk
- The bonus area on the second floor has an additional 758 square feet of living area
- 2-car side entry garage

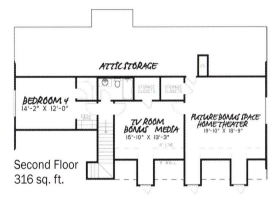

Second Floor
316 sq. ft.

ATTIC STORAGE

BEDROOM 4
14'-2" X 12'-0"

TV ROOM
BONUS MEDIA
15'-10" X 13'-3"

FUTURE BONUS SPACE
HOME THEATER
19'-10" X 18'-9"

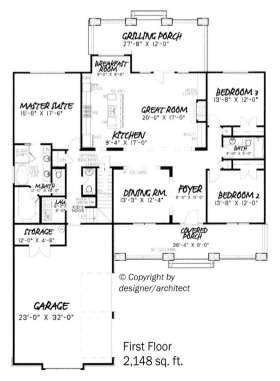

GRILLING PORCH
27'-8" X 12'-0"

BREAKFAST ROOM
9'-0" X 9'-0"

MASTER SUITE
15'-8" X 17'-6"

GREAT ROOM
20'-0" X 17'-0"

KITCHEN
9'-4" X 17'-0"

BEDROOM 3
13'-8" X 12'-0"

BATH
8'-0" X 5'-0"

M.BATH
12'-0" X 16'-0"

DINING RM.
13'-3" X 12'-4"

FOYER
8'-0" X 13'-0"

BEDROOM 2
13'-8" X 12'-0"

STORAGE
12'-0" X 4'-8"

COVERED PORCH
36'-4" X 8'-0"

© Copyright by designer/architect

GARAGE
23'-0" X 32'-0"

First Floor
2,148 sq. ft.

Images provided by designer/architect

Plan #F13-028D-0112

Dimensions:	56' W x 52' D
Heated Sq. Ft.:	1,611
Bedrooms: 3	Bathrooms: 2
Exterior Walls:	2" x 6"

Foundation: Floating slab standard; monolithic slab, crawl space, basement or walk-out basement for an additional fee

See index for more information

Features

- This Craftsman one-story home has timeless farmhouse appeal
- A cozy great room with fireplace has built ins on each side for added storage and style
- The kitchen and dining area enjoy a snack bar, great when entertaining in the great room
- The master bedroom enjoys its privacy, and its own bath and walk-in closet
- Two additional bedrooms share the full bath between them
- 2-car side entry garage

Images provided by designer/architect

houseplansandmore.com

Plan #F13-011D-0627

Dimensions:	52' W x 61' D
Heated Sq. Ft.:	1,878
Bedrooms: 3	**Bathrooms:** 2
Exterior Walls:	2" x 6"

Foundation: Crawl space or slab standard; basement for an additional fee

See index for more information

Features

- Upon entering the foyer flanked by benches, there is a soaring 16' ceiling allowing for plenty of natural light to enter the space
- Beautiful family-friendly design with a centrally located great room, dining room and kitchen combination and the sleeping quarters in a private wing
- The master suite is complete with the amenities of a walk-in closet, a double-bowl vanity and separate tub and shower units in the private bath
- Enjoy outdoor living on the covered rear patio that has a built-in barbecue grill and cabinets for ease when cooking outdoors
- 2-car front entry garage

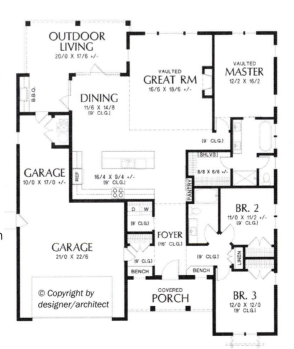

Images provided by designer/architect

Plan #F13-091D-0510

Dimensions: 76' W x 60'2" D
Heated Sq. Ft.: 2,125
Bonus Sq. Ft.: 427
Bedrooms: 3   **Bathrooms:** 2½
Exterior Walls: 2" x 6"
Foundation: Crawl space standard; slab, basement, daylight basement or walk-out basement for an additional fee

See index for more information

Images provided by designer/architect

Optional
Second Floor
427 sq. ft.

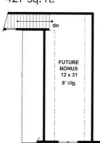

FUTURE
BONUS
12 x 31
8' clg.

© Copyright by
designer/architect

First Floor
2,125 sq. ft.

Plan #F13-026D-2134

Dimensions: 38' W x 55' D
Heated Sq. Ft.: 1,387
Bedrooms: 2   **Bathrooms:** 2
Foundation: Basement standard; crawl space, slab or walk-out basement for an additional fee

See index for more information

Images provided by designer/architect

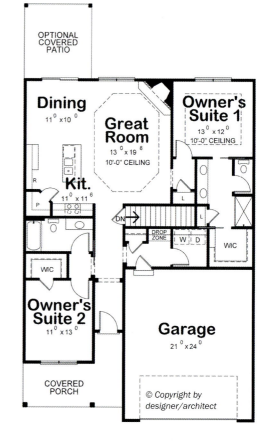

© Copyright by
designer/architect

Optional
Second Floor
812 sq. ft.

GAME ROOM
37'-4" X 18'-8"

ATTIC STORAGE

BATH

Plan #F13-055D-0162

Images provided by designer/architect

Dimensions: 84' W x 55'6" D
Heated Sq. Ft.: 1,921
Bonus Sq. Ft.: 812
Bedrooms: 3   **Bathrooms:** 2
Foundation: Crawl space or slab standard; basement or daylight basement for an additional fee

See index for more information

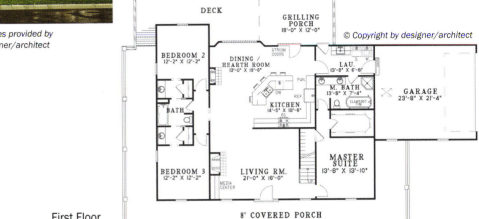

© Copyright by designer/architect

First Floor
1,921 sq. ft.

DECK

GRILLING PORCH
18'-0" X 12'-0"

BEDROOM 2
12'-2" X 12'-2"

DINING / HEARTH ROOM
13'-0" X 18'-6"

LAU.
13'-4" X 6'-0"

GARAGE
23'-8" X 21'-4"

KITCHEN
14'-5" X 18'-6"

M. BATH
13'-8" X 7'-4"

BATH

BEDROOM 3
12'-2" X 12'-2"

LIVING RM.
21'-0" X 16'-0"

MASTER SUITE
13'-8" X 13'-10"

MEDIA CENTER

8' COVERED PORCH

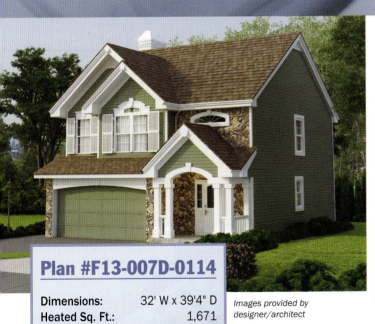

Plan #F13-007D-0114

Images provided by designer/architect

Dimensions: 32' W x 39'4" D
Heated Sq. Ft.: 1,671
Bedrooms: 3   **Bathrooms:** 2½
Foundation: Basement standard; crawl space or slab for an additional fee

See index for more information

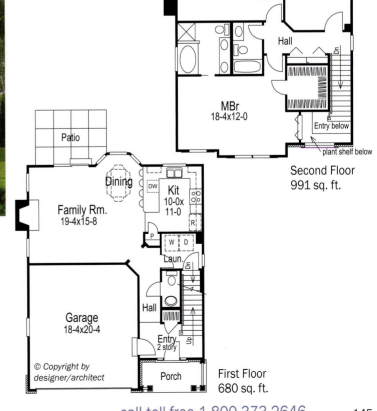

Br 2
13-7x11-3

Br 3
11-0x13-0

Hall

MBr
18-4x12-0

Entry below

plant shelf below

Second Floor
991 sq. ft.

Patio

Dining

Family Rm.
19-4x15-8

Kit
10-0x 11-0

Laun.

Garage
18-4x20-4

Hall

Entry
2 story

Porch

© Copyright by designer/architect

First Floor
680 sq. ft.

Plan #F13-056D-0110

Dimensions:	84'10" W x 61' D
Heated Sq. Ft.:	2,360
Bonus Sq. Ft.:	2,357
Bedrooms: 2	**Bathrooms:** 2
Foundation:	Basement standard; crawl space or slab for an additional fee

See index for more information

Images provided by designer/architect

© Copyright by designer/architect

First Floor
2,000 sq. ft.

Optional
Second Floor
417 sq. ft.

Lower Level
360 sq. ft.

Plan #F13-007D-0162

Dimensions:	47'8" W x 47'4" D
Heated Sq. Ft.:	1,519
Bedrooms: 4	**Bathrooms:** 2
Foundation:	Crawl space standard; basement or slab for an additional fee

See index for more information

Images provided by designer/architect

© Copyright by designer/architect

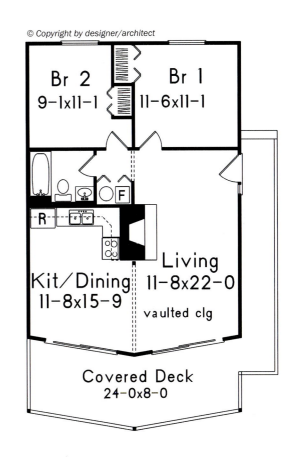

Br 2
9-1x11-1

Br 1
11-6x11-1

Kit/Dining
11-8x15-9

Living
11-8x22-0
vaulted clg

R
F

Covered Deck
24-0x8-0

Plan #F13-008D-0153

Dimensions: 24' W x 42' D
Heated Sq. Ft.: 792
Bedrooms: 2   **Bathrooms:** 1
Foundation: Crawl space standard;
slab for an additional fee

See index for more information

Images provided by designer/architect

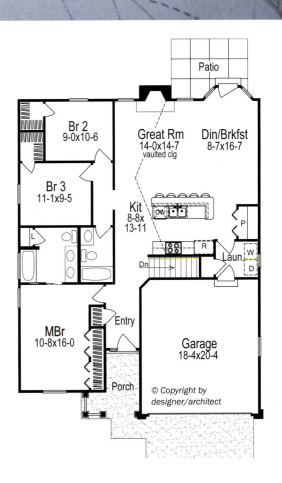

Patio

Br 2
9-0x10-6

Great Rm
14-0x14-7
vaulted clg

Din/Brkfst
8-7x16-7

Br 3
11-1x9-5

Kit
8-8x
13-11

Laun

Dn

MBr
10-8x16-0

Entry

Porch

Garage
18-4x20-4

Plan #F13-007D-5060

Dimensions: 38' W x 48'4" D
Heated Sq. Ft.: 1,344
Bedrooms: 3   **Bathrooms:** 2
Foundation: Basement standard;
crawl space or slab for an
additional fee

See index for more information

Images provided by designer/architect

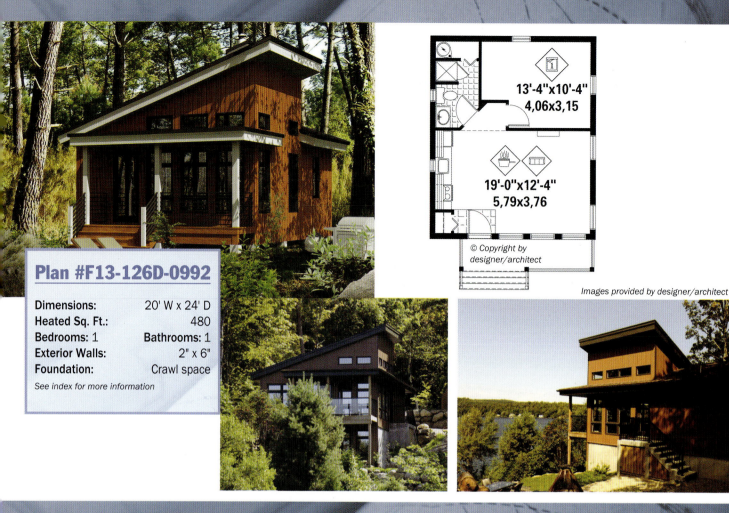

Images provided by designer/architect

Plan #F13-126D-0992

Dimensions:	20' W x 24' D
Heated Sq. Ft.:	480
Bedrooms: 1	Bathrooms: 1
Exterior Walls:	2" x 6"
Foundation:	Crawl space

See index for more information

13'-4"x10'-4"
4,06x3,15

19'-0"x12'-4"
5,79x3,76

© Copyright by designer/architect

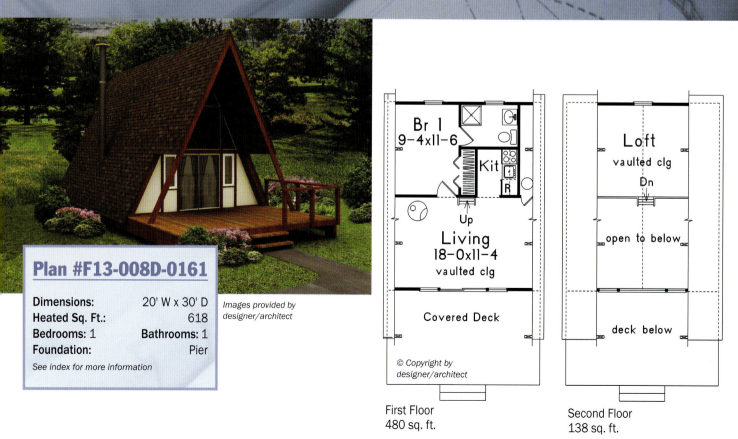

Plan #F13-008D-0161

Dimensions:	20' W x 30' D
Heated Sq. Ft.:	618
Bedrooms: 1	Bathrooms: 1
Foundation:	Pier

See index for more information

Images provided by designer/architect

Br 1
9-4x11-6

Kit

Living
18-0x11-4
vaulted clg

Covered Deck

© Copyright by designer/architect

First Floor
480 sq. ft.

Loft
vaulted clg
Dn

open to below

deck below

Second Floor
138 sq. ft.

Plan #F13-007D-0163

Dimensions: 50'8" W x 50'4" D
Heated Sq. Ft.: 1,580
Bedrooms: 3 **Bathrooms:** 2
Foundation: Crawl space standard; slab or basement for an additional fee

See index for more information

Images provided by designer/architect

© Copyright by designer/architect

Patio

Patio

MBr
15-0x13-0
vaulted

Great Room
14-0x20-5
vaulted

Dine
11-0x11-8

Multi-Purpose
8-6x9-6

Kit
14-6x10-0

DW

P

R

Laun.

D W

Hall

Entry

Br 2
11-3x10-0

Br 3
11-1x10-0
vaulted

Garage
19-4x20-4

Porch

L

Plan #F13-032D-1160

Dimensions: 49' W x 36' D
Heated Sq. Ft.: 3,258
Bedrooms: 4 **Bathrooms:** 3
Exterior Walls: 2" x 6"
Foundation: Basement standard; crawl space, floating slab or monolithic slab for an additional fee

See index for more information

Images provided by designer/architect

© Copyright by designer/architect

PATIO
17'-0" X 12'-0"

DINING ROOM
10'-0" X 13'-6"

LIVING ROOM
13'-4" X 13'-2"
CATHEDRAL CEILING

MASTER BATH
7'-6" X 13'-6"

WALK-IN
5'-0" X 9'-10"

MASTER BEDROOM
10'-8" X 13'-6"

LAUNDRY ROOM
10'-8" X 5'-6"

KITCHEN
10'-2" X 11'-2"

10'-8" X 5'-0"

FOYER
8'-0" X 6'-4"

OFFICE
10'-8" X 9'-4"

BEDROOM #2
11'-0" X 11'-6"

STOOP
10'-8" X 4'-0"

First Floor
1,629 sq. ft.

MEDIA ROOM
23'-0" X 13'-2"

BEDROOM #3
10'-0" X 13'-2"

BEDROOM #4
11'-0" X 13'-2"

PLAY ROOM
20'-3" X 16'-8"

DEN
10'-8" X 10'-0"

EXERCISE ROOM
10'-4" X 13'-0"

STORAGE
10'-8" X 9'-6"

Lower Level
1,629 sq. ft.

Second Floor
947 sq. ft.

Plan #F13-111D-0095

Dimensions: 46' W x 50'8" D
Heated Sq. Ft.: 2,458
Bedrooms: 3 **Bathrooms:** 3
Foundation: Slab standard; crawl space for an additional fee

See index for more information

Images provided by designer/architect

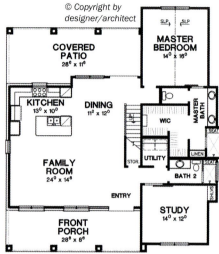

© Copyright by designer/architect

First Floor
1,511 sq. ft.

Plan #F13-121D-0010

Dimensions: 37'6" W x 52' D
Heated Sq. Ft.: 1,281
Bedrooms: 3 **Bathrooms:** 2
Foundation: Basement standard; crawl space or slab for an additional fee

Please see the index for more information

Images provided by designer/architect

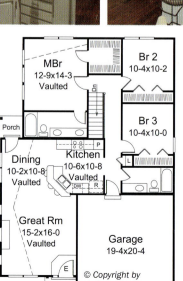

houseplansandmore.com

Plan #F13-007D-0199

Dimensions:	39' W x 33' D
Heated Sq. Ft.:	496
Bedrooms: 1	Bathrooms: 1
Foundation:	Slab

See index for more information

Images provided by designer/architect

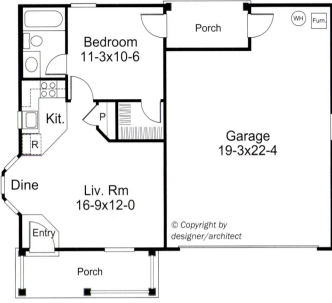

© Copyright by designer/architect

Plan #F13-013D-0134

Dimensions:	55' W x 58' D
Heated Sq. Ft.:	1,496
Bonus Sq. Ft.:	301
Bedrooms: 3	Bathrooms: 2
Foundation:	Slab standard; crawl space or basement for an additional fee

See index for more information

Images provided by designer/architect

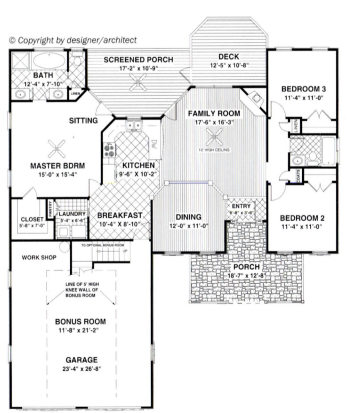

© Copyright by designer/architect

Plan #F13-169D-0003

Dimensions: 41' W x 60'4" D
Heated Sq. Ft.: 1,762
Bedrooms: 3 **Bathrooms:** 2
Foundation: Basement standard; crawl space or slab for an additional fee

See index for more information

Images provided by designer/architect

Plan #F13-013D-0156

Dimensions: 63' W x 73' D
Heated Sq. Ft.: 1,800
Bonus Sq. Ft.: 503
Bedrooms: 3 **Bathrooms:** 3
Foundation: Slab standard; crawl space or basement for an additional fee

See index for more information

Images provided by designer/architect

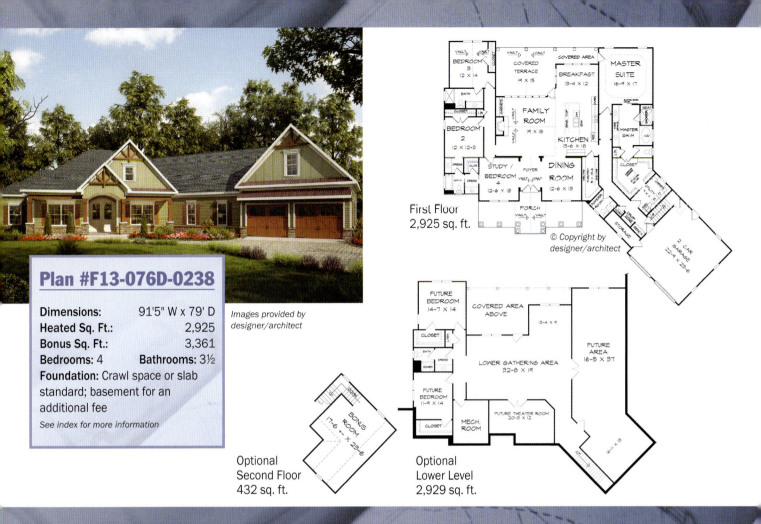

First Floor
2,925 sq. ft.

© Copyright by designer/architect

Optional
Second Floor
432 sq. ft.

Optional
Lower Level
2,929 sq. ft.

Plan #F13-076D-0238

Dimensions:	91'5" W x 79' D
Heated Sq. Ft.:	2,925
Bonus Sq. Ft.:	3,361
Bedrooms: 4	Bathrooms: 3½

Foundation: Crawl space or slab standard; basement for an additional fee

See index for more information

Images provided by designer/architect

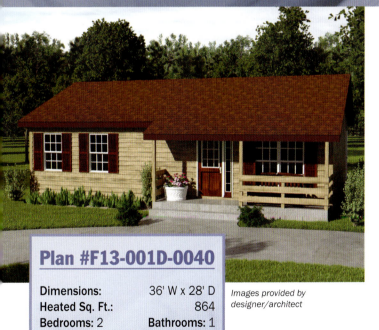

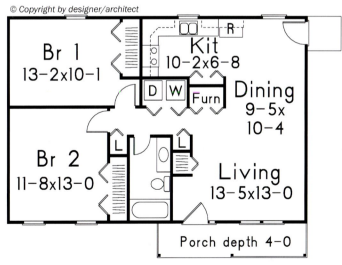

© Copyright by designer/architect

Plan #F13-001D-0040

Dimensions:	36' W x 28' D
Heated Sq. Ft.:	864
Bedrooms: 2	Bathrooms: 1

Foundation: Crawl space standard; basement or slab for an additional fee

See index for more information

Images provided by designer/architect

Plan #F13-141D-0012

Dimensions: 47' W x 46'6" D
Heated Sq. Ft.: 1,972
Bedrooms: 3   **Bathrooms:** 3½
Foundation: Crawl space standard; slab, basement or walk-out basement for an additional fee

See index for more information

Features

- An open and airy vaulted family room is adorned with a rustic stone fireplace
- The kitchen is completely open to the dining area and the great room making the entire first floor feel spacious and comfortable even when entertaining
- Covered front and back porches create plenty of outdoor living space including the second floor covered porch
- There is a master suite on the first floor as well as two additional master suites on the second floor creating plenty of living spaces for a live-in parent, or adult child

Images provided by designer/architect

First Floor
1,199 sq. ft.

© Copyright by designer/architect

Second Floor
773 sq. ft.

Plan #F13-011D-0347

Dimensions: 113'4" W x 62'8" D
Heated Sq. Ft.: 2,910
Bedrooms: 3 **Bathrooms:** 3
Exterior Walls: 2" x 6"
Foundation: Crawl space or slab standard; basement for an additional fee

See index for more information

Features

- The foyer has 11' ceilings with wood columns into the vaulted great room straight ahead
- The vaulted great room has gorgeous exposed beams, and a fireplace with built-in bookcases
- An open floor plan combines the great room, kitchen, and dining room into one big "family triangle," with no walls to cramp the space
- The kitchen has an island with a double sink, 10' ceilings, and plenty of counterspace
- 3-car side entry garage

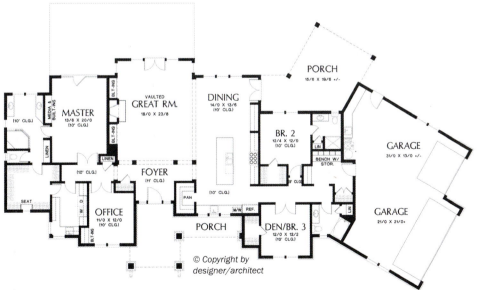

Images provided by designer/architect

Plan #F13-161D-0006

Dimensions:	82' W x 95'6" D
Heated Sq. Ft.:	4,268
Bonus Sq. Ft.:	Included
Bedrooms: 4	Bathrooms: 4½
Exterior Walls:	2" x 6"
Foundation:	Crawl space

See index for more information

Features

- What a grand entrance into this home with its vaulted beamed entry and oversized stone pillars
- The large foyer spans the width of the entry and opens into the great room with a two-story tall ceiling and centered stone fireplace
- A cozy den is located off the foyer making it easily accessible
- A built-in buffet bar is ideal for serving meals in the dining area
- Right next to the kitchen is a large walk-in pantry and half bath
- All four master bedrooms have private baths
- A convenient trash closet is located in the garage and can be accessed from the outdoors for convenience
- The rear terrace enjoys a built-in fire pit and barbecue grill
- The bonus area on the second floor is included in the square footage
- 3-car side entry garage

Images provided by designer/architect

© Copyright by designer/architect

First Floor
2,810 sq. ft.

Second Floor
1,458 sq. ft.

Images provided by designer/architect

Plan #F13-011D-0660

Dimensions:	52' W x 53' D
Heated Sq. Ft.:	1,704
Bedrooms: 3	**Bathrooms:** 2½
Exterior Walls:	2" x 6"

Foundation: Crawl space or slab standard; basement for an additional fee

See index for more information

Features

- Stylish Modern Farmhouse living has never been easier than with this perfectly-sized one-story design
- The vaulted great room has a corner fireplace and windows on two walls for an airy and open atmosphere
- A large island in the kitchen faces towards the great room and provides casual dining space
- The secluded master bedroom enjoys a large walk-in closet, and a private bath
- 2-car side entry garage

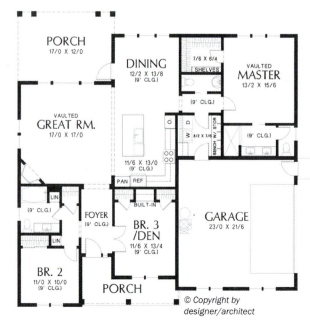

© Copyright by designer/architect

Plan #F13-032D-0932

Dimensions:	38' W x 30' D
Heated Sq. Ft.:	1,102
Bonus Sq. Ft.:	1,102
Bedrooms: 2	Bathrooms: 1
Exterior Walls:	2" x 6"

Foundation: Basement standard; crawl space, floating slab or monolithic slab for an additional fee

See index for more information

Features

- Step into the entry hall from the charming covered porch and find a walk-in closet for keeping the entry clutter-free
- The open-concept floor plan has the kitchen and dining space blending perfectly with the main living area
- The kitchen has an L-shape and features an island with dining space and a walk-in pantry with a barn door for a rustic modern farmhouse feel
- The bedroom enjoys close proximity to the pampering bath that features a shower as well as a free-standing tub in one corner
- A vaulted beamed ceiling tops the great room, dining and kitchen for a spacious, open feel you will love
- Two bedrooms share the full bath between that features both a tub and a walk-in shower
- The optional lower level has an additional 1,102 square feet of living area

First Floor
1,102 sq. ft.

Optional Lower Level
1,102 sq. ft

© Copyright by designer/architect

Images provided by designer/architect

looking inside today's best
smart homes

Since the beginning of time, interest in making life easier has always brought curiosity to inventors as well as architects. Even as far back as the Victorian era homebuilders included "dumbwaiters" in homes. Similar to an elevator but on a smaller scale that often used pulleys, a dumbwaiter was an easy method to help homeowners move things from one floor to another. So, it comes as no surprise that homeowners are still constantly searching for ways to make life easier. Whether the gadget or appliance is small such as the Crockpot in the 60s and 70s, or the Keurig® of today, we are always yearning for the latest technology to tackle life's everyday hassles with better ease.

Today's gadgets and smart home features are more seamless than ever. Most are now powered by an app that can be downloaded onto your tablet or smart phone allowing your home to be managed even while you're away. Often these added conveniences are time-saving, but they also provide better safety and health benefits. If you're interested in incorporating smart features into your new home, there are many innovative options available to homeowners and the market is continuing to grow.

Page 160, left: Google Nest Hub, store.google.com; right: Amazon Echo, amazon.com; Page 161, clockwise from top right: Ecobee thermostats help you save up to 26% on annual heating and cooling costs through advanced occupancy sensing technology, ecobee.com; GE Z-Wave Wireless Smart Lighting Control Appliance Module works with Amazon Alexa, amazon.com; Quirky + GE Aros Smart Window Air Conditioner, amazon.com; The Smart Bridge and Lutron App for Caséta Wireless are the perfect foundations for creating a connected home system, casetawireless.com; Nest Learning Thermostat, store.nest.com.

command attention

From automated lock systems to apps that manage the temperature on your thermostat, tech companies have responded to the homeowner's need for a central command hub. A hub device is designed to allow you to control all of the various apps managing functions throughout your home in one master application. Some of the top hubs on the market today include: Google Echo, Samsung SmartThings (smartthings.com), Iris Smart Hub® (lowes.com), Staples Connect™ (staples.com), and Wink (homedepot.com). If you're a homeowner that's also a tech junkie, then seamlessly managing all of your apps and home functions in one central hub really cuts down on the app clutter and confusion.

Other wireless options include Wi-Fi plug modules. GE's appliance module plugs into the wall, then plug any small appliance into the module and it instantly goes wireless and can be managed from your smart phone. There are also in-wall outlets that make the outlets themselves app-adjustable. Don't ever fear again that you left the curling iron on, and you won't be home for hours. Yes, there's now an app for that!

home basics 101

Digital thermostats, such as the ones from Nest®, sync with an app on your smart phone and even learn your habits. Then, they program themselves to turn up the temperature, or turn it down based on your routine. The Ecobee4 has a responsive display, a remote sensor and tons of smart integrations, including a built-in Amazon Alexa speaker, making it unmatched on the market.

Or, install Quirky + GE Aros Smart Air Conditioner that responds to commands from your smart phone and also uses GPS to turn itself on and off depending on where you are, resulting in money and energy savings.

Ceiling fans have also gone high tech. The Vizia RF +® Fan Speed Control (leviton.com) can adjust a fan to any speed, turn it off, set it to start at a certain time, and can also coordinate with light dimmers all while using Wi-Fi.

Control the amount of light throughout your home and the intensity with app controlled light dimmers. Some great options on the market include: Lutron Caseta® Wireless In-Wall Dimmer, left (homedepot.com), Aspire RF with Z-Wave® Dimmer (staples.com), and Leviton DZMX Z-Wave Dimmer (leviton.com). If you're interested in other smart lighting options, then the Philips Hue Wireless Dimming Kit is a simple and affordable way to get started.

Tech is even moving outdoors and getting in on the smart stuff with the Skydrop™ sprinkler system that reviews the local weather forecasts to determine watering needs and adjusts its settings accordingly. It includes both automatic and manual modes, and now works with Nest®.

interior decor

Windows, Blinds & Shades

Control the amount of light that enters your home even remotely with shades from Bali or Serena. Or, automate your shades so that as the sun shifts in the sky, the shades adjust for better efficiency and privacy.

Flooring

From cutting edge carpets to floor textiles, some new flooring options are able to track your every move and even show you the way. Lauzon Pure Genius® Smart Floor breaks down airborne contaminants. Activated by light, Pure Genius® flooring works on its own and acts as if having 3 trees inside your home. Natural or artificial light activates the titanium dioxide in Pure Genius®, setting the air-purifying agent in motion. The flooring is triggered by movement, whether from movement through a room, or a fan. The active nanoparticles in Pure Genius® decompose toxic contaminants in the air (formaldehyde and other pollutants) and convert them into harmless water and carbon dioxide molecules. Toto's Hydrotect Tile has a special coating that's antimicrobial and repels oil and dirt. So, cleaning the floor just got a whole lot faster and easier. A house coated in HydroTect purifies the same amount of air as a forest the size of four tennis courts, or decomposes the same amount of pollution produced by 30 cars driving a little over 18 miles a day.

Home Accessories

You spend more time in bed than anywhere else in your home. So why not invest in a smart bed? Sensors in the Sleep Number Mattress using their SleepIQ® Technology (sleepnumber.com) communicate with a corresponding app that calculates your breathing, heart rate, and frequency of movement. Then, outfit your smart bed with the Outlast® Temperature Regulating Sheets System that absorbs and releases excess body heat and moisture, so no need to steal, or kick the blankets off all night long anymore.

engage your senses

Today's homeowners are interested in living cleaner lifestyles free of chemicals and allergens trapped within their home. Becoming less popular are unnatural chemical laden room freshening sprays and deodorizers and taking their place are aromatherapy diffusers. These diffusers can be adjusted to run for any period of time and they use natural essential oils to eliminate odors, relieve stress, or discourage germs.

A method for monitoring home air quality is placing smoke and carbon monoxide detectors around your home. Now, these devices send your phone alerts and communicate with other units. Some distinguish between smoke and carbon dioxide and even tell you where the problem lies in a human voice. If you're concerned with water leaks and mold, then a Wally Sensor (wallyhome.com) can send you alerts about leaks and mold. A WallyHome Multi-Sensor detects and alerts you of water leaks, temperature and humidity changes, and when doors and windows open.

If you love having live plants and flowers around your home, but hate not knowing how to keep them thriving, then the Click and Grow Smartpot (clickandgrow.com) was created just for you. It dispenses the correct amount of water and nutrients for up to a month making it also great for those who travel frequently. Or, use a Parrot® Flower Power (global.parrot.com) and place the sensor into the soil and it will tell you exactly how to tend to the plant via your smart phone.

Page 162, top: Skydrop™ Smart Watering Sprinkler Controller has 8 built-in zones using the most advanced technology that accesses local weather data, calculates water, and adjusts watering schedules helping you spend less money, skydrop.com; Lauzon Pure Genius® flooring, lauzon.com; Page 163, top: i10 with Flex-Fit 3 and Sleep IQ®, sleepnumber.com; middle: Your WallyHome Sensor connects your home and keeps you informed through text message, email, push notifications or phone calls, wallyhome. com; bottom: The Click and Grow Smartpot enables you to grow fresh herbs, fruits and flowers with zero effort, clickandgrow.com.

Let yourself wake up in a more peaceful state thanks to the Yantouch Diamond+ Speaker and Alarm *(yantouch.com)*. This unique device washes the wall in soft light in millions of colors and wakes you up with sunrise hues all while playing accompanying music. Or, if drifting off to sleep tends to be more of a problem for you, then use a Drift™ Light by Saffron *(drift-light.com)*, which functions as a normal bulb until you flip the switch twice, then it softly fades in 37 minutes, which is the average time of a sunset. The bulb's warm light also induces melatonin production, which naturally controls your body's sleep and wake cycles.

Even your bathroom can be outfitted with amazing smart features such Bluetooth speaker capabilities built right into your bathtub. The Kaskade Freestanding Tubby Carver *(carvertubs.com)* can be retrofitted with Bluetooth speakers when ordered. Shower controls can also be set and regulated so the water is the optimal temperature or, sing along with your favorite playlist right inside your shower with Kohler's Moxie™ shower-head with removable speaker by Harman Kardon.

Page 164, top: Yantouch Diamond+ world's first Music+Light LED Lifestyle Bluetooth Speaker, yantouch.com/diamond; middle: Carver Tubs's Kaskade Freestanding can be retrofitted with Bluetooth speakers when ordered, carvertubs.com; left: Moxie™ shower head with built-in Harman Kardon speaker, us.kohler.com; Page 165, top, left and right: Crock-Pot® 6-Quart Smart Slow Cooker with WeMo® App, Item #SC-CPWM600-V2, crock-pot.com; middle, right: Samsung French Door Refrigerator with Family Hub™, samsung.com; Middle, left: 782 Taylor TemPerfect™ Floating Thermometers, taylor-enviro.com; Bottom: Dacor Wi-Fi Enabled Wall Oven can be controlled from an app, dacor.com.

no excuse for the perfect meal

Kitchen gadgets and appliances have come a long way and almost make it impossible to ruin a meal. For instance, there's no longer a need to hang by the oven or stove when cooking thanks to a kitchen thermometer that will ping you via an app when the meat you're cooking in the oven reaches the correct temperature. So, you can finally enjoy spending time with family and friends on the patio before dinner is served thanks to this handy device.

Or, upgrade your Crockpot to the Crock-Pot® 6-Quart. Smart Slow Cooker with WeMo® *(crock-pot.com)*. It monitors and adjusts the time and temperature remotely and will send you a notification to your smart phone when the set time has finished.

Taylor's TEMPerfect™ Floating Rings indicate a liquid's ideal temperature for poaching, simmering or boiling. Or, try their butter dish that changes color when the butter reaches room temperature.

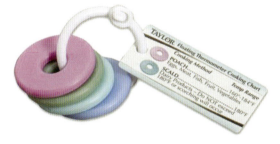

innovative home appliances

Refrigerators

Sub-Zero's® IT-36CIID Refrigerator and Freezer *(subzero-wolf.com)* uses NASA technology and includes an air purifier that rids the inside of mold and bacteria every 20 minutes. Another popular option great for busy families is the Samsung® Smart Hub Refrigerator that has a large touchscreen that lets you leave notes, view other family members' schedules, order groceries, play music, and even watch TV. It also has three cameras on the inside that can take a picture and email it to you every time you close the door. Now you can stop guessing if you need milk when grocery shopping.

Ovens

Dacor's Discovery™ iQ Wall Oven *(dacor.com)* not only screams fun since it's available in a variety of colors, but it can be controlled via Wi-Fi and features an LCD screen where you can access recipes.

Stoves

Samsung's Flex Duo™ Front Control Slide-in Dual Fuel Range with Smart Dial, Air Fry, and Wi-Fi in Black Stainless Steel is an affordable choice that connects via Wi-Fi to your smart phone so cooking dinner is effortless.

Washers & Dryers

The Whirlpool® Smart Front-Load Washer and Dryer sends alerts making you aware of peak energy-using hours and connects to your Amazon account so you can order laundry supplies easily.

other top-notch smart home electronics

Televisions

The Roku™ TV comes with fully integrated streaming and works with gaming consoles and other devices to provide hundreds of channels and platforms like Netflix™.

Sound Systems

BeoLab18 speaker towers, left *(bang-olufsen.com)* operate on a frequency that's not affected by other wireless networks. So, gone are the days of having a song stop right in the middle, or showing other signs of interference with static. You will be able to enjoy crystal clear uninterrupted sound.

Monitoring Systems

Fido feeling lonely? Then, Petcube *(petcube.com)* may be the answer. Place the cube where your pet stays when you aren't home and it streams video to your tablet or smart phone. Or, monitor your pet with Petzi Treat Cam® *(petzi.com)*, which is similar to the Petcube, but instead of a laser that plays with your pet, it dispenses treats.

If outdoor security is your interest, then SkyBell's® video doorbell quality is terrific, and integrations with Alexa, Nest®, and If This Then That (IFTTT) help it stand out in an increasingly competitive market. It also includes free online video storage and a resolution of 1080p, which are also major pluses.

Page 166, top: Samsung Flex Duo™ Range has Wi-Fi connectivity, samsung.com; middle: Bang Olufsen's BeoLab 18 speakers deliver exceptional wireless sound, and placement flexibility, bang-olufsen.com; bottom: Petcube's Bites 2 Lite Camera allows you to see, talk to, fling treats and reward your pet to enhance training and prevent anxious behavior, petcube.com.

Robots

Amazon's Astro Robot follows you from room to room playing your favorite music, podcasts or shows, and finds you to deliver calls, reminders, alarms, and timers set with Alexa. Jibo *(myjibo.com)* recognizes faces, learns your tastes, gives you reminders and communicates with you using sound effects and graphics.

Robot vacuums are one of the most popular gadgets that make cleaning less of a chore. These machines are only getting better with some that now even mop.

And, don't protect these fancy gadgets and electronics the old-fashioned way with a standard surge protector, use the Wink Pivot Surge Protector, which of course is Wi-Fi enabled.

With homeowners constantly being bombarded by alerts, messages, notifications, texts and emails, it's easy to see why gadgets and devices that reduce the amount of clutter electronically are the latest rage in home design. Incorporating these smart products into your new home will take it into the future and generally make life easier from the minute you move in. Stop wasting time and let these savvy tech items run your household like a champ; giving you more time to relax and enjoy life.

quirky finds

- Porkfolio *(wink.com)* is a piggy bank that tracks your savings and deposits, and helps you set goals. And, you can actually drop in coins and its snout lights up!

- Nokia's Body+ Health Mate Body Composition Wi-Fi Scale (health.nokia.com) monitors your weight, BMI, body fat percentage and heart rate.

- GlowCap® *(nanthealth.com/vitality)* is a pill bottle lid that reminds you to take your medicine by lighting up. It shares information with your doctor and submits prescription refills.

- Petnet iO Smartfeeder schedules pet feeding times, manages portions, and sends notifications right to your phone.

Page 167, clockwise from top: Amazon's Astro Robot follows you and plays music, makes calls, sends messages, and gets information instantly, amazon.com; Porkfolio Piggy bank uses the Wink app to monitor the amount of change you've put into its belly and track your savings goals, wink.com; Nokia's Body+ Health Mate Body Composition Wi-Fi Scale centralizes your health information to help you achieve your health goals, health.nokia.com; Vitality Glowcap® syncs with an app and reminds you to take your medicine by lighting up the cap, nanthealth.com/vitality; The Petnet iO SmartFeeder is an automatic pet feeder that dispenses food on a schedule, petnet.io.

Plan #F13-007D-0105

Dimensions: 35' W x 40'8" D
Heated Sq. Ft.: 1,084
Bedrooms: 2   **Bathrooms:** 2
Foundation: Basement standard;
crawl space or slab for an
additional fee

See index for more information

*Images provided by
designer/architect*

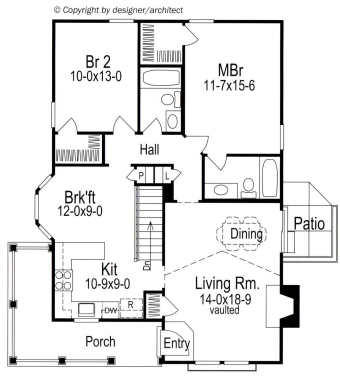

Plan #F13-001D-0086

Dimensions: 28' W x 30' D
Heated Sq. Ft.: 1,154
Bedrooms: 3   **Bathrooms:** 1½
Foundation: Crawl space standard;
slab or basement for an
additional fee

See index for more information

*Images provided by
designer/architect*

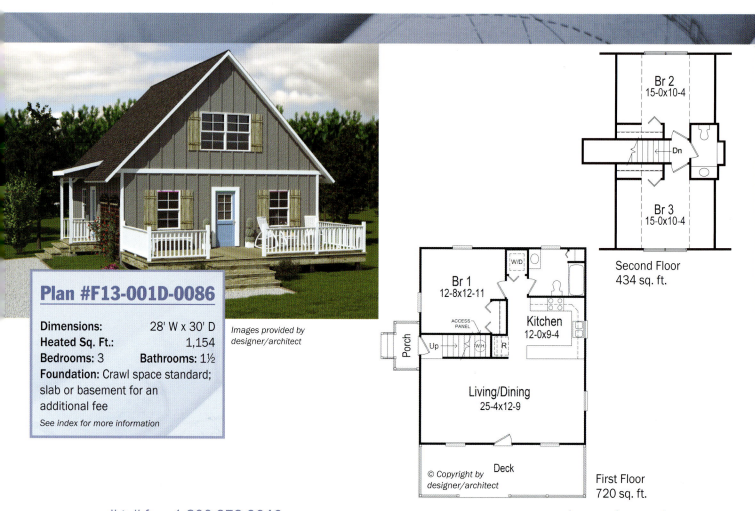

BATH
11'-5"x5'-10"

DN

STOR.
4'-3"x6'-4"

BEDROOM 2
11'-5"x8'-0"

SITTING AREA
7'-8"x10'-9"

BEDROOM 3
11'-5"x8'-0"

Second Floor
438 sq. ft.

Plan #F13-177D-0007

Dimensions:	15' W x 32' D
Heated Sq. Ft.:	918
Bedrooms: 3	**Bathrooms:** 2

Foundation: Slab standard; crawl space or basement for an additional fee

See index for more information

Images provided by designer/architect

BATH

M. CL.

STORAGE

UP

PNTY.

COVERED PATIO

PRIMARY BEDROOM
8'-11"x8'-2"

KITCHEN
11'-6"x10'-7"

FAMILY ROOM
10'-4"x10'-7"

© Copyright by designer/architect

First Floor
480 sq. ft.

Plan #F13-001D-0088

Dimensions:	32' W x 25' D
Heated Sq. Ft.:	800
Bedrooms: 2	**Bathrooms:** 1

Foundation: Crawl space standard; slab for an additional fee

See index for more information

© Copyright by designer/architect

MBr
10-4x12-1

Kit/Din
11-6x12-1

Furn

R

W
D

Br 2
13-2x8-8

Living
15-6x12-0

Porch

Images provided by designer/architect

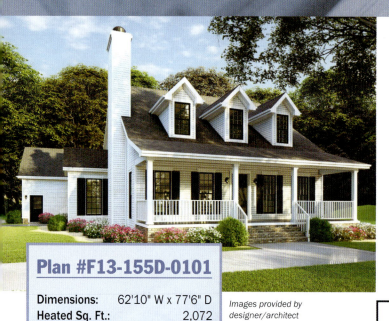

Plan #F13-155D-0101

Dimensions: 62'10" W x 77'6" D
Heated Sq. Ft.: 2,072
Bonus Sq. Ft.: 1,144
Bedrooms: 4   **Bathrooms:** 2½
Foundation: Crawl space or slab standard; basement or daylight basement for an additional fee

See index for more information

Images provided by designer/architect

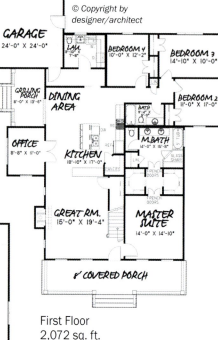

© Copyright by designer/architect

GARAGE 24'-0" X 24'-0"
LAU.
BEDROOM 4 10'-0" X 12'-2"
BEDROOM 3 14'-10" X 10'-0"
GRILLING PORCH 8'-0" X 13'-6"
DINING AREA
BEDROOM 2 11'-0" X 11'-0"
BATH 9'-4"
OFFICE 8'-8" X 11'-0"
KITCHEN 18'-10" X 17'-0"
M.BATH 14'-0" X 15'-8"
GREAT RM. 15'-0" X 19'-4"
MASTER SUITE 14'-0" X 14'-10"
8' COVERED PORCH

First Floor
2,072 sq. ft.

PROPOSED GAME ROOM.
33'-2" X 37'-6"

Optional Second Floor
1,144 sq. ft.

Plan #F13-028D-0057

Dimensions: 33' W x 36' D
Heated Sq. Ft.: 1,007
Bedrooms: 2   **Bathrooms:** 1
Foundation: Floating slab standard; monolithic slab, crawl space, basement or walk-out basement for an additional fee

See index for more information

Images provided by designer/architect

CLO. 8'-0" X 6'-6"
LAUNDRY 9'-8" X 6'-6"
STOR
MASTER BEDROOM 13'-0" X 16'-6"
KITCHEN 12'-0" X 10'-0"
LINEN
SNACK BAR
BEDROOM 2 13'-0" X 10'-0"
GREAT ROOM 20'-0" X 14'-0"
© Copyright by designer/architect
COVERED PORCH

MBr
14-0x11-8

Br 2
10-0x9-2

W/D

Br 3
10-0x9-10

Living
14-0x18-9

Patio

Kit
8-0x11-0

Din

Entry

WH   F

Garage
19-4x20-4

Porch

© Copyright by
designer/architect

Plan #F13-007D-0108

Dimensions: 25' W x 60' D
Heated Sq. Ft.:   983
Bedrooms: 3   **Bathrooms:** 2
Foundation: Crawl space standard;
slab for an additional fee

See index for more information

*Images provided by
designer/architect*

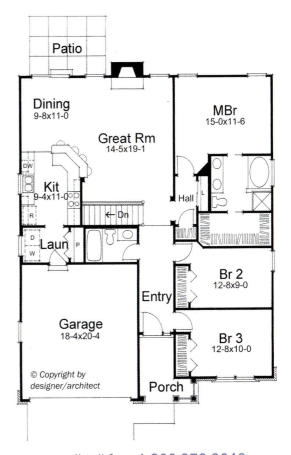

Patio

Dining
9-8x11-0

Great Rm
14-5x19-1

MBr
15-0x11-6

DW

Kit
9-4x11-0

Hall   L

Dn

Laun   P

Br 2
12-8x9-0

D
W

Entry

Br 3
12-8x10-0

Garage
18-4x20-4

Porch

© Copyright by
designer/architect

Plan #F13-147D-0001

Dimensions: 40'8" W x 49'4" D
Heated Sq. Ft.:   1,472
Bedrooms: 3   **Bathrooms:** 2
Foundation: Basement standard;
crawl space or slab for an
additional fee

See index for more information

*Images provided by
designer/architect*

Plan #F13-001D-0013

Dimensions: 60'10" W x 51'2" D
Heated Sq. Ft.: 1,882
Bedrooms: 3   **Bathrooms:** 2
Foundation: Basement standard; crawl space or slab for an additional fee

See index for more information

Images provided by designer/architect

Plan #F13-013D-0133

Dimensions: 36' W x 42'4" D
Heated Sq. Ft.: 953
Bedrooms: 2   **Bathrooms:** 1½
Foundation: Crawl space standard; basement or slab for an additional fee

See index for more information

Images provided by designer/architect

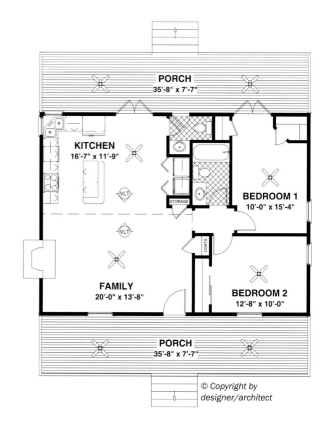

© Copyright by designer/architect

Plan #F13-003D-0005

Dimensions: 80' W x 42' D
Heated Sq. Ft.: 1,708
Bedrooms: 3   **Bathrooms:** 2
Foundation: Basement standard; crawl space or slab for an additional fee

See index for more information

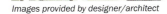

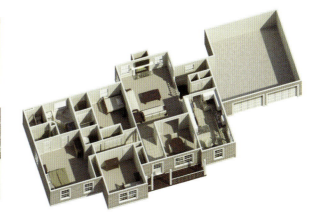

Images provided by designer/architect

Second Floor
621 sq. ft.

First Floor
1,404 sq. ft.

© Copyright by designer/architect

Plan #F13-065D-0448

Dimensions: 50' W x 45' D
Heated Sq. Ft.: 2,025
Bonus Sq. Ft.: 1,404
Bedrooms: 4   **Bathrooms:** 2½
Foundation: Basement standard; crawl space, slab or walk-out basement for an additional fee

See index for more information

Images provided by designer/architect

Optional
Lower Level
1,404 sq. ft.

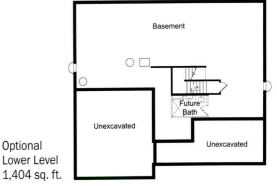

Plan #F13-032D-0935

Dimensions:	24' W x 24' D
Heated Sq. Ft.:	1,050
Bedrooms: 2	**Bathrooms:** 1½
Exterior Walls:	2" x 6"

Foundation: Basement standard; crawl space, monolithic slab or floating slab for an additional fee

See index for more information

Images provided by designer/architect

Second Floor
474 sq. ft.

© Copyright by designer/architect

First Floor
576 sq. ft.

Plan #F13-016D-0105

Images provided by designer/architect

Dimensions:	81'3" W x 63'8" D
Heated Sq. Ft.:	2,065
Bedrooms: 3	**Bathrooms:** 2½

Foundation: Crawl space or slab standard; basement for an additional fee

See index for more information

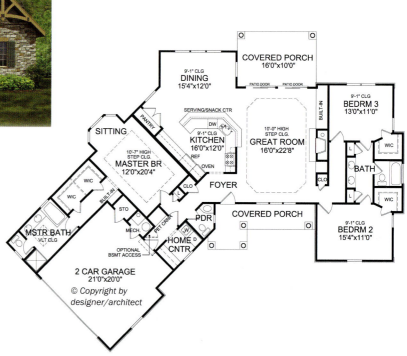

Second Floor
699 sq. ft.

© Copyright by
designer/architect

*Images provided by
designer/architect*

Plan #F13-036D-0240

Dimensions:	55' W x 52'8" D
Heated Sq. Ft.:	2,557
Bonus Sq. Ft.:	248
Bedrooms: 3	Bathrooms: 2½
Foundation:	Slab

See index for more information

First Floor
1,858 sq. ft.

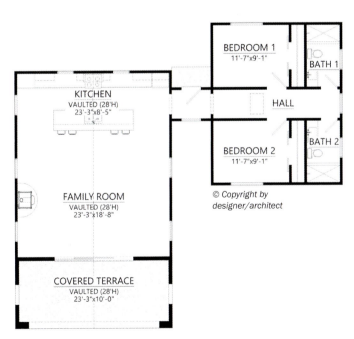

© Copyright by
designer/architect

Plan #F13-177D-0008

*Images provided by
designer/architect*

Dimensions:	50' W x 45' D
Heated Sq. Ft.:	1,192
Bedrooms: 2	Bathrooms: 2
Foundation:	Slab

See index for more information

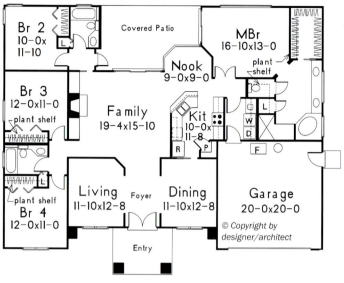

Plan #F13-048D-0008

Dimensions:	61'8" W x 50'4" D
Heated Sq. Ft.:	2,089
Bedrooms: 4	**Bathrooms:** 3
Foundation:	Slab

See index for more information

Images provided by designer/architect

© Copyright by designer/architect

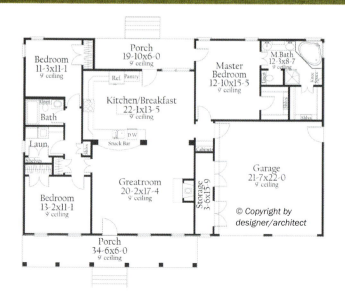

Plan #F13-084D-0065

Dimensions:	60' W x 44' D
Heated Sq. Ft.:	1,633
Bedrooms: 3	**Bathrooms:** 2

Foundation: Crawl space or slab standard; basement for an additional fee

See index for more information

Images provided by designer/architect

© Copyright by designer/architect

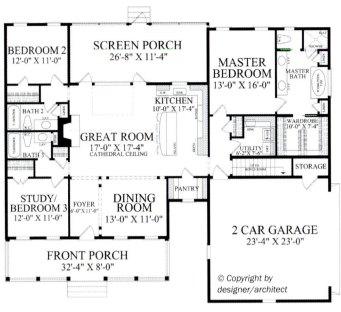

Plan #F13-128D-0313

Dimensions: 64'2" W x 52'2" D
Heated Sq. Ft.: 1,903
Bedrooms: 3   **Bathrooms:** 3
Foundation: Basement or crawl space, please specify when ordering

See index for more information

Images provided by designer/architect

BEDROOM 2
12'-0" X 11'-0"

SCREEN PORCH
26'-8" X 11'-4"

MASTER BEDROOM
13'-0" X 16'-0"

MASTER BATH

BATH 2

BATH 3

KITCHEN
10'-0" X 17'-4"

GREAT ROOM
17'-0" X 17'-4"
CATHEDRAL CEILING

WARDROBE
10'-0" X 7'-4"

UTILITY
6'-2" X 7'-6"

STORAGE

STUDY/
BEDROOM 3
12'-0" X 11'-0"

FOYER
6'-0" X 11'-0"

DINING ROOM
13'-0" X 11'-0"

PANTRY

2 CAR GARAGE
23'-4" X 23'-0"

FRONT PORCH
32'-4" X 8'-0"

© Copyright by designer/architect

Plan #F13-058D-0267

Dimensions: 60' W x 38' D
Heated Sq. Ft.: 1,280
Bedrooms: 3   **Bathrooms:** 2
Foundation: Basement

See index for more information

Images provided by designer/architect

Garage
19-8x25-4

© Copyright by designer/architect
16'x7' Door

Kit/Brk
16-4x15-1

Pantry

MBr
11-6x12-2

Lndry
5-5x7-6

Family
16-4x15-11

Bedrm 3
10-0x10-6

Bedrm 2
10-0x10-6

Porch
16-8x6-4

Plan #F13-065D-0446

Dimensions:	50'6" W x 58' D
Heated Sq. Ft.:	2,094
Bonus Sq. Ft.:	1,425
Bedrooms: 4	Bathrooms: 2½
Foundation:	Basement

See index for more information

Second Floor
669 sq. ft.

First Floor
1,425 sq. ft.

© Copyright by designer/architect

Optional
Lower Level
1,425 sq. ft.

Images provided by designer/architect

Plan #F13-065D-0429

Images provided by designer/architect

Dimensions:	60' W x 55'1" D
Heated Sq. Ft.:	1,867
Bonus Sq. Ft.:	1,867
Bedrooms: 3	Bathrooms: 2½
Foundation:	Basement

See index for more information

First Floor
1,867 sq. ft.

© Copyright by designer/architect

Optional
Lower Level
1,867 sq. ft.

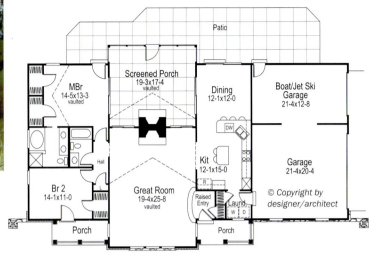

Plan #F13-007D-0137

Dimensions: 72'8" W x 44'4" D
Heated Sq. Ft.: 1,568
Bedrooms: 2   **Bathrooms:** 2
Foundation: Crawl space standard; slab for an additional fee

See index for more information

Images provided by designer/architect

Plan #F13-011D-0677

Dimensions: 38' W x 72' D
Heated Sq. Ft.: 1,922
Bedrooms: 3   **Bathrooms:** 2
Exterior Walls: 2" x 6"
Foundation: Crawl space or slab standard; basement for an additional fee

See index for more information

Images provided by designer/architect

Plan #F13-013D-0235

Dimensions: 71'2" W x 64'6" D
Heated Sq. Ft.: 2,140
Bonus Sq. Ft.: 1,535
Bedrooms: 3   Bathrooms: 3
Foundation: Crawl space standard; slab or basement for an additional fee

See index for more information

Images provided by designer/architect

Optional Second Floor 1,535 sq. ft.

First Floor 2,140 sq. ft.

© Copyright by designer/architect

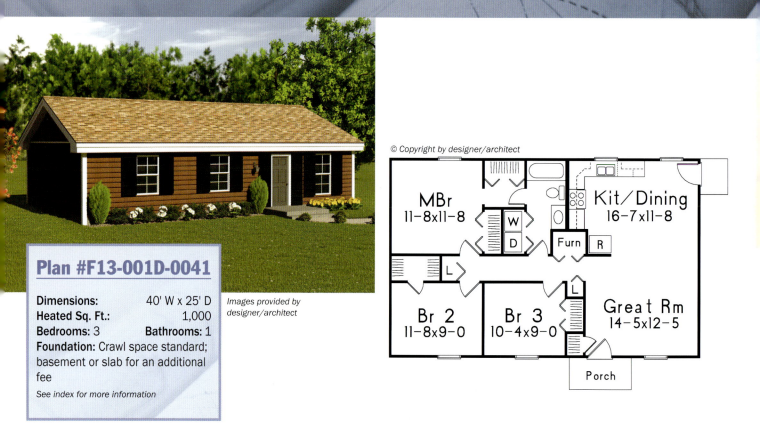

Plan #F13-001D-0041

Dimensions: 40' W x 25' D
Heated Sq. Ft.: 1,000
Bedrooms: 3   Bathrooms: 1
Foundation: Crawl space standard; basement or slab for an additional fee

See index for more information

Images provided by designer/architect

© Copyright by designer/architect

Second Floor
950 sq. ft.

Plan #F13-164D-0004

Dimensions: 93'8" W x 76'11" D
Heated Sq. Ft.: 3,273
Bedrooms: 5 **Bathrooms:** 4½
Foundation: Slab

See index for more information

Images provided by designer/architect

© Copyright by designer/architect

First Floor
2,323 sq. ft.

Images provided by designer/architect

Plan #F13-172D-0045

Dimensions: 66' W x 50'6" D
Heated Sq. Ft.: 1,972
Bonus Sq. Ft.: 2,030
Bedrooms: 3 **Bathrooms:** 2
Exterior Walls: 2" x 6"
Foundation: Walk-out basement standard; monolithic slab, stem wall slab, crawl space, daylight basement or basement for an additional fee

See index for more information

Optional Lower Level
2,030 sq. ft.

© Copyright by designer/architect

First Floor
1,972 sq. ft.

Plan #F13-011D-0759

Dimensions:	29' W x 48' D
Heated Sq. Ft.:	1,056
Bedrooms: 2	**Bathrooms:** 2
Exterior Walls:	2" x 6"

Foundation: Crawl space or slab standard; basement for an additional fee

See index for more information

Features

- An open and airy vaulted living room is adorned with a fireplace
- The kitchen is open to the dining area and the living room making the entire first floor feel spacious and comfortable even when entertaining
- Covered front and back porches create plenty of outdoor living space
- The bedrooms are split from one another for added privacy

© Copyright by designer/architect

PORCH
29/0 X 8/0
(232 SQ. FT.)

14/2 X 9/2+/-
(10' CLG.)

REF
PAN
LIN
T·W·H

BR. 1
11/0 X 13/0
(10' CLG.)

DINING
12/0 X 9/6
(10' CLG.)

W/D

TILE
SHWR

SLOPE UP

VAULTED
LIVING
16/8 X 14/0

SLOPE UP

LINEN
5/6x3/6

PORCH
17/0 X 6/0
(102 SQ. FT.)

BR. 2
11/0 X 11/0
(10' CLG.)

Images provided by designer/architect

HOME PLANS INDEX

why buy
STOCK PLANS?

Building a home yourself presents many opportunities to showcase your creativity, individuality, and dreams turned into reality. With these opportunities, many challenges and questions will crop up. Location, size, and budget are all important to consider, as well as special features and amenities. When you begin to examine everything, it can become overwhelming to search for your dream home. But, before you get too anxious, start the search process an easier way and choose a home design that's a stock home plan.

Custom home plans, as well as stock home plans, offer positives and negatives; what is "best" can only be determined by your lifestyle, budget, and time. A customized home plan is one that a homeowner and designer or architect work together to develop from scratch, taking ideas and putting them down on paper. These plans require extra patience, as it may be months before the architect has them drawn and ready. A stock plan is a pre-developed plan that fits the needs and desires of a group of people, or the general population. These are often available within days of purchasing and typically cost up to one-tenth of the price of customized home plans. They still have all of the amenities you were looking for in a home, and usually at a much more affordable price than having custom plans drawn for you.

When compared to a customized plan, some homeowners fear that a stock home will be a carbon copy home, taking away the opportunity for individualism and creating a unique design. This is a common misconception that can waste a lot of money and time!

As you can see from the home designs throughout this book, the variety of stock plans available is truly impressive, encompassing the most up-to-date features and amenities. With a little patience, browse the numerous available stock plans available throughout this book, and easily purchase a plan and be ready to build almost immediately.

Plus, stock plans can be customized. For example, perhaps you see a stock plan that is just about perfect, but you wish the mud room was a tad larger. Rather than go through the cost and time of having a custom home design drawn, you could have our customizing service modify the stock home plan and have your new dream plan ready to go in no time. Also, stock home plans often have a material list available, helping to eliminate unknown costs from developing during construction.

It's often a good idea to speak with someone who has recently built. Did they use stock or custom plans? What would they recommend you do, or do not undertake? Can they recommend professionals that will help you narrow down your options? As you take a look at plans throughout this publication, don't hesitate to take notes, or write down questions. Also, take advantage of our website, houseplansandmore.com. This website is very user-friendly, allowing you to search for the perfect house design by style, size, budget, and a home's features. With all of these tools readily available to you, you'll find the home design of your dreams in no time at all, thanks to the innovative stock plans readily available today that take into account your wishes in a floor plan as well as your wallet.

how can I find out if I can AFFORD to build a home?

The most important question for someone wanting to build a new home is, "How much is it going to cost?" You must have an accurate budget before ordering house plans and beginning construction, or your dream home will quickly turn into a nightmare. We make building your dream home a much simpler reality thanks to the estimated cost-to-build report available for all of the home plans in this book and on our website, houseplansandmore.com.

Price is always the number one factor when choosing a new home. Price dictates the size and the quality of materials you will use. So, it comes as no surprise that having an accurate building estimate prior to making your final decision on a home plan quite possibly is the most important step.

If you feel you've found "the" home, then before buying the plans, order a cost-to-build report for the zip code where you want to build. This report is created specifically for you when ordered, and it will educate you on all costs associated with building the home. Simply order the cost-to-build report on houseplansandmore.com for the home design you want to build and gain knowledge of the material and labor cost. Not only does the report allow you to choose the quality of the materials, you can also select from various options from lot condition to contractor fees. Successfully manage your construction budget in all areas, clearly see where the majority of the costs lie, and save money from start to finish.

To the right are the categories included in a cost-to-build report. Each category breaks down labor cost, material cost,

funds needed, and the report offers the ability to manipulate over/under adjustments if necessary.

BASIC INFORMATION includes your contact information, the state and zip code where you intend to build and material class. This section also includes: square footage, number of windows, fireplaces, balconies, baths, garage location and size, decks, foundation type, and bonus room square footage.

GENERAL SOFT COSTS include cost for plans, customizing (if applicable), building permits, pre-construction services, and planning expenses.

SITE WORK & UTILITIES include water, sewer, electric, and gas. Choose the type of site work and if you'll need a driveway.

FOUNDATION includes a menu that lists the most common types.

FRAMING ROUGH SHELL calculates rough framing costs including framing for fireplaces, balconies, decks, porches, basements and bonus rooms.

ROOFING includes several common options.

DRY OUT SHELL allows you to select doors, windows, and siding.

ELECTRICAL includes wiring and the quality of the light fixtures.

PLUMBING includes labor costs, plumbing materials, plumbing fixtures, and fire proofing materials.

HVAC includes costs for both labor and materials.

INSULATION includes costs for both labor and materials.

FINISH SHELL includes drywall, interi-

or doors and trim, stairs, shower doors, mirrors, bath accessories, and labor costs.

CABINETS & VANITIES select the grade of your cabinets, vanities, kitchen countertops, and bathroom vanity materials, as well as appliances.

PAINTING includes all painting materials, paint quality, and labor.

FLOORING includes over a dozen flooring material options.

SPECIAL EQUIPMENT NEEDS calculate cost for unforeseen expenses.

CONTRACTOR FEE AND / OR PROJECT MANAGER FEES includes the cost of your cost-to-build report, project manager and/or general contractor fees. If you're doing the managing yourself, your costs will be tremendously lower in this section.

LAND PAYOFF includes the cost of your land.

RESERVES AND / OR CLOSING COSTS include interest, contingency reserves, and any closing costs.

We've taken the guesswork out of figuring out what your new home is going to cost. Take control of construction, determine the major expenses, and save money. Supervise all costs, from labor to materials and manage construction with confidence, which allows you to avoid costly mistakes and unforeseen expenses. To order a Cost-To-Build Report, visit houseplansandmore.com and search for the specific plan. Then, look for the button that says, "Request Your Report" and get started.

what kind of
PLAN PACKAGE do I need?

5-SET PLAN PACKAGE includes five complete sets of construction drawings. Besides one set for yourself, additional sets of blueprints will be required for your lender, your local building department, your contractor, and any other tradespeople working on your project. Please note: These 5 sets of plans are copyrighted, so they can't be altered or copied.

8-SET PLAN PACKAGE includes eight complete sets of construction drawings. Besides one set for yourself, additional sets of blueprints will be required for your lender, your local building department, your contractor, and any other tradespeople working on your project. Please note: These 8 sets of plans are copyrighted, so they can't be altered or copied.

PDF FILE FORMAT is our most popular plan package option because of how fast you can receive them your blueprints (usually within 24 to 48 hours Monday through Friday), and their ability to be easily shared via email with your contractor, subcontractors, and local building officials. The PDF file format is a complete set of construction drawings in an electronic file format. It includes a one-time build copyright release that allows you to make changes and copies of the plans. Typically you will receive a PDF file via email within 24-48 hours (Monday-Friday, 7:30am-4:30pm CST) allowing you to save money on shipping. Upon receiving, visit a local copy or print shop and print the number of plans you need to build your home, or print one and alter the plan by using correction fluid and drawing in your modifications. Please note: These are flat image files and cannot be altered electronically. PDF files are non-refundable and not returnable.

CAD FILE FORMAT is the actual computer files for a plan directly from Auto-CAD, or another computer aided design program. CAD files are the best option if you have a significant amount of changes to make to the plan, or if you need to make the plan fit your local codes. If you purchase a CAD File, it allows you, or a local design professional the ability to modify the plans electronically in a CAD program, so making changes to the plan is easier and less expensive than using a paper set of plans when modifying. A CAD package also includes a one-time build copyright release that allows you to legally make your changes, and print multiple copies of the plan. See the specific plan page for availability and pricing. Please note: CAD files are non-refundable and not returnable.

MIRROR REVERSE SETS Sometimes a home fits a site better if it is flipped left to right. A mirror reverse set of plans is simply a mirror image of the original drawings causing the lettering and dimensions to read backwards. Therefore, when ordering a mirror reverse set of plans, you must purchase at least one set of the original plans to read from, and use the mirror reverse set for construction. Some plans offer right reading reverse for an additional fee. This means the plan has been redrawn by the designer as the mirrored version and can easily be read.

ADDITIONAL SETS You can order extra plan sets of a plan for an additional fee. A 5-set or 8-set must have been previously purchased. Please note: Only available within 90 days after purchase of a plan package.

2" X 6" EXTERIOR WALLS 2" x 6" exterior walls can be purchased for some plans for an additional fee (see houseplansandmore.com for availability and pricing).

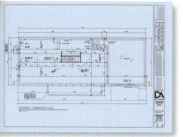
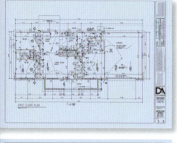
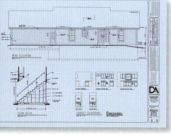
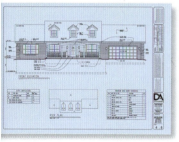

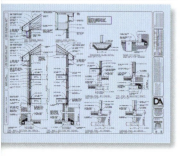

our
PLAN PACKAGES include...

Quality plans for building your future, with extras that provide unsurpassed value, ensure good construction and long-term enjoyment. A quality home - one that looks good, functions well, and provides years of enjoyment - is a product of many things - design, materials, and craftsmanship. But it's also the result of outstanding blueprints - the actual plans and specifications that tell the builder exactly how to build your home.

And with our BLUEPRINT PACKAGES you get the absolute best. A complete set of blueprints is available for every design in this book. These "working drawings" are highly detailed, resulting in two key benefits:

- **BETTER UNDERSTANDING BY THE CONTRACTOR OF HOW TO BUILD YOUR HOME AND...**
- **MORE ACCURATE CONSTRUCTION ESTIMATES THAT WILL SAVE YOU TIME AND MONEY.**

Below is a sample of the plan information included for most of the designs in this book. Specific details may vary with each designer's plan. While this information is typical for most plans, we cannot assure the inclusion of all the following referenced items. Please contact us at 1-800-373-2646 for a plan's specific information, including which of the following items are included.

1 cover sheet is included with many of the plans, the cover sheet is the artist's rendering of the exterior of the home. It will give you an idea of how your home will look when completed and landscaped.

2 foundation plan shows the layout of the basement, walk-out basement, crawl space, slab or pier foundation. All necessary notations and dimensions are included. See plan page for the foundation types included. If the home plan you choose does not have your desired foundation type, our Customer Service Representatives can advise you on how to customize your foundation to suit your specific needs or site conditions.

3 floor plans show the placement of walls, doors, closets, plumbing fixtures, electrical outlets, columns, and beams for each level of the home.

4 interior elevations provide views of special interior elements such as fireplaces, kitchen cabinets, built-in units and other features of the home.

5 exterior elevations illustrate the front, rear and both sides of the house, with all details of exterior materials and the required dimensions.

6 sections show detail views of the home or portions of the home as if it were sliced from the roof to the foundation. This sheet shows important areas such as load-bearing walls, stairs, joists, trusses and other structural elements, which are critical for proper construction.

7 details show how to construct certain components of your home, such as the roof system, stairs, deck, etc.

do you want to make
CHANGES to your plan?

We understand that sometimes it is difficult to find blueprints that meet all of your specific needs.
That is why we offer home plan modification services so you can build a home exactly the way you want it!

ARE YOU THINKING ABOUT CUSTOMIZING A PLAN?

If you're like many customers, you may want to make changes to your home plan to make it the dream home you've always wanted. That's where our expert design and modification partners come in. You won't find a more efficient and economic way to get your changes done than by using our home plan customizing services.

Whether it's enlarging a kitchen, adding a porch, or converting a crawl space to a basement, we can customize any plan and make it perfect for your needs. Simply create your wish list and let us go to work. Soon you'll have the blueprints for your new home, and at a fraction of the cost of hiring a local architect!

IT'S EASY!

- We can customize any of the plans in this book, or on houseplansandmore.com.
- We provide a FREE cost estimate for your home plan modifications within 24-48 hours (Monday-Friday, 7:30am-4:30pm CST).
- Average turn-around time to complete the modifications is typically 4-5 weeks.
- You will receive one-on-one design consultations.

CUSTOMIZING FACTS

- The average cost to have a house plan customized is typically less than 1 percent of the building costs — compare that to the national average of 7 percent of building costs.
- The average modification cost for a home is typically $800 to $1,500. This does not include the cost of purchasing the PDF file format of the blueprints, which is required to legally make plan changes.

OTHER HELPFUL INFORMATION

- Sketch, or make a specific list of changes you'd like to make on the Home Plan Modification Request Form.
- A home plan modification specialist will contact you within 24-48 hours with your free estimate.
- Upon accepting the estimate, you will need to purchase the PDF or CAD file format.
- A contract, which includes a specific list of changes and fees will be sent to you prior for your approval.
- Upon approving the contract, our design partners will keep you up to date by emailing sketches throughout the project.
- Plans can be converted to metric, or to a Barrier-free layout (also referred to as a universal home design, which allows easy mobility for an individual with limitations of any kind).

2 easy steps

1 visit

houseplansandmore.com
and click on the Resources tab at the top of the home page, then click "How to Customize Your House Plan," or scan the QR code here to download the Home Plan Modification Request Form.

2 email

your completed form to:
customizehpm@designamerica.com,
or fax it to: 651-602-5050.

If you are not able to access the Internet, please call 1-800-373-2646
(Monday-Friday, 7:30am - 4:30 pm CST).

helpful BUILDING AIDS

Your Blueprint Package will contain all of the necessary construction information you need to build your home. But, we also offer the following products and services to save you time and money during the building process.

MATERIAL LIST
Many of the home plans in this book have a material list available for purchase that gives you the quantity, dimensions, and description of the building materials needed to construct the home (see houseplansandmore.com for availability and pricing). Keep in mind, due to variations in local building code requirements, exact material quantities cannot be guaranteed. Note: Material lists are created with the standard foundation type only. Please review the material list and the construction drawings with your material supplier to verify measurements and quantities of the materials listed before ordering supplies.

THE LEGAL KIT
Avoid many legal pitfalls and build your home with confidence using the forms and contracts featured in this kit. Included are request for proposal documents, various fixed price and cost plus contracts, instructions on how and when to use each form, warranty statements and more. Save time and money before you break ground on your new home or start a remodeling project. All forms are reproducible. This kit is ideal for homebuilders and contractors. Cost: $35.00

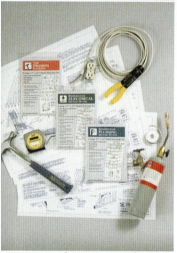

DETAIL PLAN PACKAGES - ELECTRICAL, FRAMING & PLUMBING
Three separate packages offer homebuilders details for constructing various foundations; numerous floor, wall and roof framing techniques; simple to complex residential wiring; sump and water softener hookups; plumbing connection methods; installation of septic systems, and more. Each package includes three dimensional illustrations and a glossary of terms. Purchase one or all three. Please note: These drawings do not pertain to a specific home plan, but they include general guidelines and tips for construction in all 3 of these trades. Cost: $30.00 each or all three for $60.00

EXPRESS DELIVERY
Most orders are processed within 24 hours of receipt. Please allow 7-10 business days for standard delivery. If you need to place a rush order, please call us by 11:00 am Monday-Friday, CST and ask for express service (allow 1-2 business days). Please see page 191 for all shipping and handling charges.

TECHNICAL ASSISTANCE
If you have questions about your blueprints, we offer technical assistance by calling 1-314-770-2228 (Monday-Friday, 7:30am-4:30pm CST). Whether it involves design modifications or field assistance, our home plans team is extremely familiar with all of our home designs and will be happy to help. We want your home to be everything you expect it to be.

before you ORDER

Please note: Plan pricing is subject to change without notice. For current pricing, visit houseplansandmore.com, or call us at 1-800-373-2646.

BUILDING CODE REQUIREMENTS
At the time the construction drawings were prepared, every effort was made to ensure that these plans and specifications met nationally recognized codes. These plans conform to most national building codes. Because building codes vary from area to area, some drawing modifications and/or the assistance of a professional designer or architect may be necessary to comply with your local codes, or to accommodate your specific building site conditions. We advise you to consult with your local building official, or a local builder for information regarding codes governing your area prior to ordering blueprints.

COPYRIGHT
Plans are protected under Copyright Law. Reproduction by any means is strictly prohibited. The right of building only one structure from all plan packages is licensed exclusively to the buyer and the plans may not be resold unless by express written authorization from the home designer, or architect. You may not use this plan to build a second or multiple structure(s) without purchasing a multi-build license. Each violation of the Copyright Law is punishable in a fine.

LICENSE TO BUILD
When you purchase a "full set of construction drawings" from Design America, Inc., you are purchasing an exclusive one-time "License to Build," not the rights to the design. Design America, Inc. is granting you permission on behalf of the plan's designer or architect to use the construction drawings one-time for the building of the home. The construction drawings (also referred to as blueprints/plans and any derivative of that plan whether extensive or minor) are still owned and protected under copyright laws by the original designer. The blueprints/plans cannot be resold, transferred, rented, loaned or used by anyone other than the original purchaser of the "License to Build" without written consent from Design America, Inc., or the plan designer. If you are interested in building the plan more than once, please call 1-800-373-2646 and inquire about purchasing a Multi-Build License that will allow you to build a home design more than one time. Please note: A multi-build license can only be purchased if a CAD file or PDF file were initially purchased.

EXCHANGE POLICY
Since blueprints are printed in response to your order, we cannot honor requests for refunds.

SHIPPING & HANDLING CHARGES

U.S. SHIPPING -
(AK and HI express only)
Regular (allow 7-10 business days)	$35.00
Priority (allow 3-5 business days)	$55.00
Express* (allow 1-2 business days)	$75.00

CANADA SHIPPING**
Regular (allow 8-12 business days)	$50.00
Express* (allow 3-5 business days)	$100.00

OVERSEAS SHIPPING/INTERNATIONAL
Call, fax, or e-mail (customerservice@designamerica.com) for shipping costs.

*   For express delivery please call us by 11:00am Monday-Friday, CST

** Orders may be subject to custom's fees and or duties/taxes.

Note: Shipping and handling does not apply on PDF and CAD File orders. PDF and CAD File orders will be emailed within 24-48 hours (Monday-Friday, 7:30am-4:30pm CST) of purchase.

Please send me the following:

Plan Number: F13-_____

Select Foundation Type: (Select ONE- see plan page for available options).

❏ Slab ❏ Crawl space ❏ Basement

❏ Walk-out basement ❏ Pier

❏ Optional Foundation for an additional fee

    Enter foundation cost here $ _____

Plan Package   Cost

❏ CAD File $ _____

❏ PDF File Format (recommended) $ _____

❏ 8-Set Plan Package $ _____

❏ 5-Set Plan Package $ _____

Visit houseplansandmore.com to see current pricing for all plan package options available, or call 1-800-373-2646.

Important Extras

❏ Additional plan sets*:

    _____ set(s) at $_____ per set $ _____

❏ Print in right-reading reverse:

    one-time additional fee of $_____ $ _____

❏ Print in mirror reverse:

    _____ set(s) at $_____ per set $ _____

    (where right reading reverse is not available)

❏ Material list $ _____

❏ Legal Kit (001D-9991, see page 190) $ _____

Detail Plan Packages: (see page 190)

    ❏ Framing   ❏ Electrical   ❏ Plumbing $ _____
    (001D-9992)   (001D-9993)   (001D-9994)

Shipping (see page 191) $ _____

SUBTOTAL $ _____

Sales Tax (MO residents only, add 8.24%) $ _____

TOTAL $ _____

*Available only within 90 days after purchase of plan.

Helpful Tips

- You can upgrade to a different plan package within 90 days of your plan purchase.
- Additional sets cannot be ordered without purchasing 5-Sets or 8-Sets.

Name _____

    (Please print or type)

Street _____

    (Please do not use a P.O. Box)

City _____ State _____

Country _____ Zip _____

Daytime telephone   (_____) _____

E-Mail _____

    (For invoice and tracking information)

Payment   ❏ Bank check/money order. No personal checks.

    Make checks payable to Design America, Inc.

❏ MasterCard   ❏ VISA   ❏ DISCOVER   ❏ American Express Cards

Credit card number _____

Expiration date (mm/yy) _____ CID _____

Signature _____

❏ I hereby authorize Design America, Inc. to charge this purchase to my credit card.

Please check the appropriate box:

❏ Building home for myself

❏ Building home for someone else

Order Online

houseplansandmore.com

Order By Phone

1-800-373-2646
Fax: 314-770-2226

Order By Mail

Design America, Inc.
734 West Port Plaza, Suite #208
St. Louis, MO 63146

Express Delivery

Most orders are processed within 24 hours of receipt. If you need to place a rush order, please call us by 11:00 am CST and ask for express service.

Business Hours: Monday - Friday (7:30 am - 4:30 pm CST)

Best-Selling Home Plans

SOURCE CODE **F13**